OUR TONGUES WERE LOOSED

John J. Jankauskas

OUR TONGUES WERE LOOSED

Parish Experiences in the Liturgical Renewal

The Newman Press • 1965 • Westminster, Maryland

Nihil Obstat: Rev. George J. Dyer, J.C.D.
Censor Librorum

Imprimatur: Most Rev. Cletus O'Donnell, J.C.D.
Vicar General, Archdiocese of Chicago
February 11, 1964

The nihil obstat and imprimatur are official declarations that a book or pamphlet is considered to be free from doctrinal or moral error. No implication is intended that those who have granted the nihil obstat and imprimatur agree with the contents, opinions or statements expressed.

 Library of Congress Catalog Card Number: 64-66332.

Preface

IN THE Church, it is possible to examine any serious question from a kind of two-fold aspect which embraces both a "hierarchic" pole and a "community" pole. But, indeed, the Church must examine itself from this dual aspect if it is to avoid the "ivory tower approach to the realities of life"—a thought so well developed by Yves Congar in his classic book *Lay People in the Church.*[1]

In our day we are witnessing the remarkable work of the hierarchy at Vatican II. The culmination of their work on the Liturgy resulted in a document—the Constitution on the Sacred Liturgy. But what about the community? Karl Rahner, in his book *Free Speech in the Church,*[2] stresses the importance of knowing the precise situation at hand, when it comes to the people or the immediate *community:* people's desires, feelings, emotions, worries . . . what their problems are . . . what they find difficult . . . to what extent their feelings have changed . . . where they find the traditional answers or rulings insufficient.

This is what the present work attempts to do regarding certain aspects of the Liturgy. We will look at the Liturgy, then, from a somewhat different perspective; this viewpoint is the "community" pole—that is, what is often so patronizingly referred to as the "grass-roots" approach. What does the hierarchy teach on such points of the Liturgy? What does the community of the faithful feel about those same questions? It should come as no surprise that the learned conciliar decree by

[1] Westminster, Md.: Newman, 1959.

[2] New York: Sheed and Ward, 1959.

the hierarchy, and this modest work of a group of parishioners, should complement one another even though the present work was already close to completion at the convocation of the Council. One work begins at the top and the other at the bottom, but the same Holy Spirit is at work in both places, and both are intended to arrive at the same destination, in and through this Holy Spirit.

Admittedly this is an intensive study of one parish. Yet what may seem to be uniquely ours is undoubtedly shared by all—or surely, by *many*—parishes who are struggling to improve their worship, who are looking for fresh approaches to community worship. This is in accord with the findings of a noted psychologist, Carl R. Rogers, who says " . . . that what is most personal and unique in each one of us is probably the very element which would, if it were shared or expressed, speak most deeply to others." [3]

And so, on reading some of the quotations included here, many people have found that a kind of dialogue took place with themselves: "Why, that man said just what I feel but never said." Or, "I really disagree with that one." And, "On many of these pages, I almost suspect you are quoting me."

Before any idea can become a reality in our lives, it is prerequisite for us to *identify* with the idea. Perhaps a canon lawyer can identify himself with a legal document, but for most of us this is extraordinarily difficult. Some of this difficulty, it seems to me, adheres to our present responsibility to identify with the council decree on the Liturgy. This book, then, is intended to help ordinary people, sometimes priests, sometimes laymen, to identify themselves with the decree, which is a hierarchical document, written about the community-of-the-faithful's level of approach to active participation in the Liturgy. In another sense, we will try to appeal to any person interested in finding out how other people go about their method of worshiping at Mass.

[3] *On Becoming a Person* (Boston: Houghton Mifflin, 1961), p. 26.

The reactions and emotions expressed by so many others in this book—and I can substantiate them all from much the same experience in two other big city parishes—prove that for the layman, active participation is no mere passing fancy by any twisting of the imagination. Now that the Constitution on the Liturgy has given the marching orders, the clergy ought to take heart from the genuine enthusiasm expressed herein. The Council decree opens doors—to research, to challenge, to the search for grass-roots feelings, reactions, and insights. It gives direction to further studies of the Liturgy *as it is actually felt by the community*, people and priest.

It is high time to accept that challenge.

Acknowledgments

I AM deeply grateful to all who shared with me their insights and views and consented to have them published. Many persons unstintingly devoted their time and talents to typing the large number of interviews and copies of the manuscript at its various stages of completion. We would especially like to thank Marilyn Karieva, Stella Sikorcin, Noreen Young, Helen Peterson, Barbara Neilson, Zenaida Dratnol and Mary Skupien for their endless hours of typing, and several others who contributed their time and talents. We express our thanks to Arthur Harmon, Sr., who spent many hours re-checking the accuracy of the quotations used. It was indeed a privilege for me to work with all these and other dedicated people and to have been given the opportunity to be the catalyst in the production of their combined efforts to bring this work to completion.

The Author

Contents

Introduction

OBVIOUSLY, it will profit the Church to look at things from many vantage points. The vantage point of the layman is not the least of these. Christ said, "I know *mine.*" And so bishops and priests too desire to know their 'sheep,' but all too rarely do we know what is in the mind and heart of the layman—because he will almost never express himself unless we ask him. Centuries ago, St. Cyprian said plainly enough, "I would not make a decision without the consent and assent of the laity"—a sentiment echoed through those centuries and into our own times by many bishops. With this thought in mind, we dare lay bare our own awarenesses of the Mass as they appear to us. What we say we owe largely to the people who are the mind and heart of St. Rose of Lima parish.

We will take a look at the Mass with and without active participation, using a clinical and experiential approach which does not speculate on what things *might* be, or what we would want them to be, but seeks rather to discover what they actually are: What has meaning for the people? What do people *enjoy?* What bores them?

We asked laymen to express themselves freely. Often, we cite their very words, express their thoughts, draw conclusions from them. We seek, then, to find ways to make the Mass more meaningful, more alive, more effective in the lives of these people.

How can Catholics find in the Mass the strength and inspiration to Catholic action and rich Christian living, if their attitude towards the Mass is expressed in such terms as,

> Well, I was there in Church, but was I really at Mass? I fufilled my obligation . . . ?

Nor will Catholic leadership spring from the Mass when the Mass generates such descriptions as "watch the priest move around the altar"—"I'd say the rosary and look at somebody else's hat and notice who had a new dress and finally I would look at my watch and then I was out. I was through for another week"—"dull hour"—"drag."

Shall we scapegoat the laity for these reactions? Past generations of clergy? Our educational system? Or should we smugly explain them away as the materialism and secularism of our age? In any case, we cannot wholly absolve the laity from all guilt. But when great numbers of people do not find satisfaction and enjoyment in the Mass, the time has come for some serious questioning.

Priests, I believe, find it particularly difficult to have a true estimate of the value of active participation in the lives of the laity when they view it against the background of their clerical lives. A priest's experience of and attitude toward the Mass is so much different from the experience and attitudes of the laity. For example, priests barely tolerated the prayers tacked on at the end of Mass for the Conversion of Russia, and were very happy to be free of them. Many people miss them. These prayers gave them their one chance to participate after being silent spectators throughout the whole Mass. Now, it doesn't seem quite "kosher" to them that these were taken away too.

Some fine books have been written on participation from the theological, historical and clerical points of view. This is not our aim. We will attempt to look at participation from the layman's viewpoint, trying to understand his outlook. From this vantage point, we will put forth a plan for introducing and improving active participation, evolving a practical approach from the background of fourteen years of experience. Even parishes which have enjoyed participation for several years may find the insights of the laity helpful and some suggestions for improving participation beneficial. Some may feel that since they have already introduced participation, the suggested methods for introducing it are useless or of little value. What is written here may have even greater value to those parishes as a method of evaluating active participation in the parish and stimulating deeper growth and wider acceptance of it among the people.

It was the present pastor of St. Rose of Lima parish who first suggested we write this book. The idea of the book received impetus at one of our CFM meetings when one of the men popped the question as to why we had so much Latin in the Mass—that he didn't like it—and all the people began expressing themselves on this and other topics of the Mass. I tape-recorded the session and when listening to it later, it suddenly occurred to me that it was a real privilege for me to gain insight into the layman's view of participation. I began multiplying interviews with a great variety of people. The more I multiplied the interviews, the more I learned about participation. These interviews really awakened a new world for me, uncovered ideas I thought could be helpful to everyone. It is from these interviews that this book has come to be an inductive study of active participation.

Some discussions I really preferred to reproduce at great length, but instead chose to group selected quotations under various topics for the sake of clarity. We were not interested in any statistical count of the numbers for or against participation, Latin, etc., but simply sought an expression of their feelings on whatever points they mentioned.

Three hundred and eighty-three people in forty-five groups were interviewed. Each group ranged in size from six to twelve people. Some persons were individually interviewed. The breakdown according to age was as follows: Teenagers, 10%; 21-34, 44%; 35-54, 28%; over 55, 18%. According to marital status: Single, 21%; married, 74%; widows, 5%. Forty-five percent of the adults interviewed were men (155 men, 191 women).

This is a study of a good cross section of parishioners who were asked for their views on participation—admittedly inadequate for a detailed statistical analysis of active participation.

A great number of group discussions antecedent and consequent to the interviews used took place. I visited the homes of countless numbers of parishioners. There, too, I listened to expressions relative to participation, parallel to those recorded in this book. Many volunteered information to me as I greeted them after Mass in front of the church Sunday after Sunday. Others expressed themselves to the men commentators. None of this unrecorded material is part of this book although it substantiates the recorded work.

St. Rose of Lima is one of the few parishes that had participation in our archdiocese prior to the recent decrees of Pope Pius XII, Vatican Council II and our own Albert Cardinal Meyer. Our participation dates back thirteen years. It was introduced into the parish during the pastorate of the late Rev. Francis W. Glynn. It continues to flourish and mature under the present pastor, Rev. James Brian Fleming. The success of the program of participation I share with my fellow assistants, Rev. John Fearon, with whom we began participation and more recently, the Rev. Charles Ezerskis who stepped into the role of extending the program with much enthusiasm. Public statements of compliment and appreciation from visiting priests and missionaries proved very helpful and encouraging to the people. A variable factor difficult to measure, but of immeasurable importance, is the enthusiasm of priests for active participation at Mass.

The parish consists of approximately one thousand families. Within our parish boundaries, approximately one and one-half square miles, there are eight nationality parishes, two Uniate parishes, three Protestant churches and an Orthodox Church—a neighborhood where people have a choice of going to different churches. Many parishes are within walking distance for most people. It is a working-class neighborhood. Only a few professional people are numbered among our parishioners. In a parish such as St. Rose of Lima, it is a gamble when one begins anything new.

It is by the grace of God and the enthusiasm of two pastors, assistants and organists, that we have participation for these many years. If one were to pick a parish to begin active participation, one certainly would not pick the parish of St. Rose of Lima. As one man reflected: "It is the most unlikely spot in the entire archdiocese where participation would flourish. If it flourishes here, it could flourish anywhere."

OUR TONGUES WERE LOOSED

[1]

Participation by Consent

Too good to be true that the priest would ask us about our opinions. . . . It was a real honor to be asked.

DICTATORIAL methods not only lack permanence, they generate resentment. Psychological conditioning, so successful in advertising, does bring results, but you will have only a participated activity among the laity—a participating crowd, but not a worshiping people.

Father, quit imposing participation on the people!

I confess I failed in many ways regarding the introduction and promotion of active participation at Mass in our parish. My failure was due not to a lack of interest or conviction regarding the value of participation, but rather to the somewhat military approach which I used in instituting it.

I imposed participation on the people. Picture a sergeant barking orders: " ---- ------------ --- ---------- ------!" Only this time I was the "sergeant" facing the "company" of parishioners in the "fieldhouse" of St. Rose of Lima Church. "Sing this hymn!" "Answer this prayer!" "Receive Holy Communion!"

It is quite a shock to discover one's sincerest efforts backfiring. "*Sing*, men!" But some would not sing. "Pick up your Mass cards"—many left them in the pews. "Take part in the Mass"—some rosaries dangled even more pronouncedly. "Answer the priest aloud"—a few heads burrowed deeper into prayerbooks or missals. A few even walked away and worship no more in our Church. People resent orders. Commands backfire.

In this, I suppose I was no different from most priests. Generally speaking, this is the way we have been treating people. It's so easy to stand there in the pulpit, present plans and issue orders. The approaches to building a new church, asking for donations, pushing a new parish organization or calling attention to spiritual obligations differ little. We tell them what we want them to do. And we expect their ready cooperation: indeed, we clobber any resentment with a firm appeal to their loyalty and spirit of obedience to the Church. In other words, we *demand* obedience, blind cooperation—perhaps not in so many words, but obviously in effect.

Yet some parishioners found no objection to my early methods and attribute to them the success of the whole program, as the following excerpt of a conversation with a parishioner illustrates:

> Ten years ago you imposed participation on the people. This was the success of your program. If you had not insisted, it would not be there. You just pounded away at it until the people felt they could no longer fight you, so they might as well join you.

No matter how kind and approving this and similar statements by parishioners are, I cannot help but interpret them in the light of the traditional attitude of people toward a priest. Many parishioners excuse our methods and swallow their resentments. At best, we priests can say they simply tolerate our approach. Parishioners obey, carry out our suggestions, eventually discovering their true worth (when there). When our methods fail, oftentimes we lash out in our hearts and in our sermons at our parishioners—at our hardhearted people, so stubborn, so uncooperative, so critical. It's easy to justify one's efforts and scapegoat the people for our failures; yet we find God speaking to us through his mysterious Presence in our parishioners. The Holy Spirit speaks to us through their very hardheadedness, their stubbornness, their non-cooperation, their criticism. Yes, it is so easy to blindfold one's eyes or close one's ears and refuse to listen to the voice of the Holy Spirit manifested in the reactions of our parishioners. Priests should therefore reject as inadequate any approach which appeals to the virtue of obedience and blind cooperation in parishioners.

Oftentimes failures force us to search for new methods. We must launch out to the discovery of new approaches. Even the United States Army is changing its training tactics. Sometimes to our surprise, the new is really very old, so human, so adult and so successful. Our personal struggles lead us now to recommend a method of introducing and developing participation drawn from two founts—St. Thomas and his treatise on prudence, so clearly put forth by Fr. Charles Curran in his book, *Counseling in Catholic Life and Education*,[1] and psychological studies on participation in industry and related fields. In reality, we are looking at one approach from two aspects, theological and psychological.

To accomplish our aim of adult participation, we recommend a positive, constructive, *adult* approach:

1. Model the approach on the mode of the Holy Spirit who acts on all souls by way of counsel.
2. Activate the prudential process in every parishioner.
3. Involve all the parish in the very actions of introducing participation to the fullest possible extent.

Really, this approach merely patterns the action of God's grace. God does not act by way of command—but by counsel.

> It is proper to the rational creature to be moved through the research of reason to perform any particular action, and this research is called counsel. Hence the Holy Ghost is said to move the rational creature by way of counsel.[2]

[1] New York: Macmillan & Co., 1957.

[2] Summa, II-II AE, q. 52, art. 1.

> So great is his respect for our freedom that his own mastery gives way before it.[3]

God respects our freedom. God permits us to say no. Similarly when priests are presenting participation to the people they must offer them the opportunity to make a choice and the right to say *no*. If participation is as reasonable and good as we say it is, need we fear that the people will not rationally and freely choose it?

Blindly to participate simply because the pastor tells us to participate is not an act of virtue. Nor does passive obedience generate enthusiastic *adult* active participation. Forcing a person to abandon past prayer habits at Mass either through gentle prodding or rigid jarring does not release the emotional hold on those prayer habits, but triggers off a more open display of negative feelings toward active participation. The stronger the force, the tighter the grip. A person must examine, in the clear light of reason, fixed attitudes which he has carried over from the past, and then freely abandon them. A person must be able to say: "I choose to do so, not because you say so, but because I see it for myself as the better, more reasonable, manner of action."

St. Thomas calls this rational examination and choice leading to action the *prudential process.*

> Prudence is right reason applied to action. It involves three steps—first to take counsel, second to judge what one has discovered and the third is to command.[4]

Prudence is thus a *personal* virtue, residing in the person who undertakes an action. More accurately stated, the first stage of prudence is a personal inquiry—a self-exploration—a personal survey into the means and methods to reach our goals, the information gathering stage by the individual undertaking

[3] Yves M. Congar, O.P., *Lay People in the Church* (Westminster, Md.: Newman Press, 1959), p. 416.

[4] Summa, D. II-II, q. 47, a. 8.

the action. The inquiry stage operates in two ways. A person either learns through self-discovery of necessary facts, or acquires information from another which must be integrated and made part of his personal inquiry.

Once all the needed information is gathered, the second stage of prudence is entered—the self-judgment stage. A person judges: "This is the right course of action." He charts a particular plan of action.

This leads to the third stage of prudence—self-command. A person orders himself to action. He executes what he has selected to be the right course of action.

A wife aptly illustrated the prudential process in operation in her relationship with her husband: "I will listen to what he says" (self-inquiry stage, integrating the information or counsel she receives from her husband into her personal survey), "make up my own mind" (on the right course of action—self-judgment stage), "then, I will do what *I* decide is right" (self-command stage).

The presentation of participation to the parish must neither ignore nor dispense with the prudential process, but rather must strive to activate it. It will be helpful to study the application of the prudential process to active participation in a more detailed way.

The Self-Inquiry Stage

A parishioner is already aware of his past manner of attending Mass. Perhaps he loved to finger his rosary, page through his prayerbook, wrap himself in the Sunday Missal, or just simply gaze about with occasional attempts at personal prayer. All of these methods have meaning for him, deep meaning on occasion—experiences he treasures, graces he remembers receiving, personal favors granted through such prayers. He has a deep emotional attachment to such methods of "participating" at Mass. He is very much aware of many feelings attached to such prayer. Perhaps he might even have some knowledge of active participation. However, more than likely, information about active participation at Mass will be missing. It is the rôle of the priest to supply this information. He explains what active participation is, its effects, its values—the new and fruitful way of entering into the Mystery of the Mass. The parishioner integrates the new information into his store of knowledge. All this then becomes part of his personal *survey:* his personal awareness of the different ways of attending Mass and their values for him.

The Self-Judgment Stage

We leave to each parishioner the right to make his own judgment as to his course of action regarding his participation at Mass. We will not make the decision for him. He must be free to select his manner of attending Mass. We must, in short, be "Catholic" enough to make room for everybody.

The Self-Command Stage

The parishioner's manner of participating at Mass will follow his self-judgment, his choice. Some will reject active participation at Mass. Others will try it and see it in actuality, wishing to explore the question further before passing final judgment. Many will freely commit themselves to it. There is a real and legitimate joy and satisfaction in exercising one's freedom of choice of action.

We can bear in mind these words of Pius XII when we are introducing participation:

> The people and a shapeless multitude (or as it is called "the masses") are two distinct concepts. The people lives and moves by its own life energy: the masses are inert of themselves and can only be moved from outside. The people lives by the fullness of life in the men that com-

> pose it, each of whom—at his proper place and in his own way—is a person conscious of his own responsibility and of his own views. The masses, on the contrary, wait for the impulse from the outside, an easy plaything in the hands of anyone who exploits their instincts and impressions, ready to follow, in turn, today this flag, tomorrow another.[5]

Even though Pius XII's words apply directly to the danger of mass acquiescence regarding the political and social order, they do have a bearing on the manner of our relating to people and introducing participation. There can be no doubt that we can get a mass acceptance of participation through the use of advertising techniques and psychological conditioning, moving the people through external motivation, but—let us ask again—would we have a worshiping people, or just a participating crowd? The impulse to participate must not come from outside the person, but must come from inner conviction; must be the result of the prudential process, a free action—a free *commitment* on the part of each person. These words of Pius XII must come alive at Mass. Each person, on his own responsibility, must actively commit himself to participation in the Mass. This is our goal.

It is only thus that we will have true, active participation.

To this end, we might consider the conclusions of several recent psychological studies on participation in fields such as industry which possess ready application to active participation at Mass.

> When the individual goes through motions that he does not find meaningful, when he does not really participate, then comes rebellion against authority, complaints, griping, gossip, rumors, scapegoating, dissatisfaction of all sorts. The job satisfaction is low. In McGregor's terms, the individual is not active, he is industrially reactive . . .

[5] Christmas Message, 1944.

> A person ceases to be reactive and contrary in respect to a desirable course of conduct only when he himself has had a hand in declaring that course of conduct to be desirable. Such findings add up to the simple proposition that people must have a hand in saving themselves; they cannot and will not be saved from the outside.[6]

> When a person is deprived of his sense of individual participation and responsibility, it seems to destroy his enthusiasm and consistency in carrying out any joint projects.[7]

We can safely conclude that at least some of the opposition to active participation is due to the lack of active involvement of the parishioners in the very action of introducing it. When parishioners are not given a hand in the introduction of active participation, we can say that some become *re*active to it. We must give them a rôle in the very instituting of it. Individual participation and individual responsibility create enthusiasm.

There is also a certain joy and satisfaction in exercising responsibility for originating something. How often have we found greater satisfaction in making something, rather than in enjoying the finished product? Sometimes there is more joy to a housewife in the long cooking than in actually eating the meal. A youngster often enjoys making a model plane more than he does playing with it once it is made.

In other words, everyone takes pride in his own work. No one rejects or abandons his own child. The institution of active participation in a parish must become the "child" of the entire parish. If the whole parish is creating something, the whole parish is proud of that something.

[6] Gordon W. Allport, "The Psychology of Participation," address given at the annual meeting of the Society for the Psychological Study of Social Issues at Columbia University, September 16, 1944, published in *Psychological Review,* Vol. 53 (May, 1945) pp. 122-123.

[7] Charles Curran, *Counseling in Catholic Life and Education* (New York: Macmillan & Co., 1957) p. 371.

Once a person makes his choice, he usually stands by it even in the face of disillusionment. We are loyal to our choices. We are enthusiastic about that which we had a hand in making. No one shares the enthusiasm of the original creator unless he somehow re-creates it and improves it. Even priests would receive less grudgingly regulations and projects from the bishop, and would carry them out more enthusiastically—if they had a hand in making them. Similarly, parishioners more readily accept active participation in the Church when they have part in its very institution.

We cannot approach participation as a miracle drug newly concocted, a ready-made pill for the pastor to administer and for the people to swallow, thus effecting a miraculous transformation of parishioners into dynamic Catholics. Rather participation is like a new product to be synthesized by the whole parish like a team of chemists—searching, inventing, experimenting. Perhaps the greatest and most profound value comes from the participation of the parishioners in its development. The artist, the builder and the composer get greater joy and satisfaction than do those who admire and use their works.

How do we translate the principles of the prudential process of St. Thomas and the psychology of participation into a practical program?

Active participation aims at changing silent spectators, passive observers, into vocal participants, persons attentive and alive to the public prayer of the Church. However, active participation cannot be limited to saying "Et cum spiritu tuo" and "Amen." It must go beyond the ritual, sacrificial participation. Passivity at Mass merely externalizes the much deeper passivity that usually permeates a man's total relationship to the Church. Failure to involve people actively when introducing participation is to contradict the very spirit of active participation and ignore this equally harmful passivity towards the Church. In this light, the people become playthings in the hands of the pastor, as if they had no minds or wills of their own. Before he expected them to be silent. He permitted them to pray personally. Now, suddenly, he expects them to speak out at Mass, to pray publicly on cue.

More than once priests will explain the greeting "Dominus vobiscum" and "Et cum spiritu tuo" as an expression of solidarity between priest and people in offering the sacrifice. Why not have the people feel this solidarity with the priest as we bring about active participation? The priest will expect the people to say "Amen" to the great sacrificial action of the Mass: Why not have them say "Amen" to the very project of introducing active participation in the Church? In this way, it becomes possible to counteract the ritual passivity that is the all too ordinary fate of people at Mass.

Most people will agree that if you can involve a group actively in an undertaking, you will have a great possibility of success, and surely an enthusiastic response. Just how can a pastor do this? More pointedly, how can priests treat people as adults and not as children? How can we bring about participation without laying it flat on the line and saying, "Well, here it is, you have to take it. Go on, swallow it. . . . It's *good* for you." Not unlike giving medicine to children.

It is vital to a democracy to give the community a say-so. Furthermore, a little democracy goes a long way. It helps avoid opposition and creates enthusiasm; it pays rich dividends. Priests, especially, should welcome the idea of active involvement of every person in the parish in the introduction of participation. It stands to reason that different individuals will be involved to different degrees in this action. Nevertheless, the entire parish must experience the active involvement in this project to some degree, even the minutest, or somebody is taking an unjustifiable—and unchristian—chance with the success of the project.

Now, in the practical application of these principles, we do not want to leave the impression that the suggested detailed outline is the only possible application of the prudential process in this area of introducing and evaluating participation. The following pages can be considered more as an illustration rather than as a rigid guide. Each parish must discover the prudential process coming alive in the parish in a unique way which the priest and people will surprisingly discover. What is important is the basic attitude and orientation of the prudential process, understanding, etc. The priest first divides the parish into three groups. The first group consists of people who participate in the parish through parochial organizations of one kind or another. The second group consists of people who come to Mass on Sundays, but take no part in the parish organizations. The third group is composed of the people who rarely, if ever, go to Mass, but who still consider themselves Catholics—and parishioners.

The first group can be reached through the regular meetings of the particular organization. The second group can only be reached through Sunday sermons. The priest's only contact with the third group is through a letter or, far better, a personal visit.

He might begin by creating an atmosphere of interest with a bulletin announcement such as:

> TIME OF DECISION DRAWS NEAR——Next Sunday on the front page of this bulletin, a topic will be presented that will affect the lives of all parishioners for many years to come.

The following Sunday, the topic of active participation can be introduced with another more challenging bulletin announcement:

> TIME OF DECISION——This is a decision that will affect all our lives: active participation at Mass through group singing, group praying, group responding to the priest's prayer at the altar.
> You may find this an interesting topic of dis-

> cussion with your family, among your friends, with your neighbors.
> Opportunities will be provided for every parishioner to voice his opinions, to share his views.
> This parish will NOT launch out into a full-scale program of active participation at Mass without the consent of the people!
>
> Participation with the consent of the people may be disturbing to some. What if the people do not assent to the program of active participation at Mass? Fine. What better proof that the people are not ready for active participation at Mass! A more extensive educational program is called for; a deeper, lengthier period of preparation is required.

The priests in every parish rely very much on those people who participate in the parish organizations to carry out their parochial programs. Certainly the intention is not to antagonize this group in any way, but rather win their active enthusiastic support. We here entrust them with an active role —a *very* active one—in introducing participation. The basic movement is one of discussion—group discussion.

First, a priest should not pre-decide his plans of bringing about active participation. He should not tell the parishioners what to do. He ought not say, "*I* want to bring about participation"; or "*I* want you to participate in the Mass." What to do, then?

One procedure is to *depersonalize* the regulations of the Church, the wish of the Holy Father, or the regulations of the chancery office. A suggested opening for such a discussion:

> *The Constitution on the Sacred Liturgy* states: "Mother Church earnestly desires that all the faithful should be led to that full, conscious, and active participation in liturgical celebrations which is demanded by the very nature of the liturgy. . . . In the restoration and promotion of the sacred liturgy, the full and active participation by all the people is the aim to be considered

> before all else; for it is the primary and indispensable source from which the faithful are to derive the true Christian spirit. . . ."[8]

or:

> Our Cardinal wrote in a pastoral letter: "I wish to encourage all our parishes and institutions, in the spirit of obedience to the wishes of the Holy See, to promote as fully as possible the norms laid down in the 1958 Instruction of the Sacred Congregation of Rites.
>
> "We want, as much as possible, to have our people enter into the Mass as a corporate act of worship and not simply for private devotion."[9]

We parish priests, the "administrative" wing, do not identify ourselves either with the council, the pope or even the bishop. Once we have presented the directive, we can open the discussion: "We wonder how you feel about active participation. If you feel it is a good thing, how should we go about beginning it in our parish? What do you think we ought to do? Feel free to express yourselves, your opinions. Perhaps some of you have questions you would like to ask."

Catch the basic movement? Priests are not telling the people that *we are going to have* participation. Priests ask for their opinions, their suggestions. Priests want them to feel a real part of this project. Priests want to involve them all. It is important that priests be sensitive to people's feelings in this regard, whether in opposition or support. Sometimes just the expression of feelings of opposition decreases their intensity. Priests must listen to their opinions and their suggestions. It is a very good idea to have a secretary take notes of what is said. More than likely, many things of significant value will be expressed. A sense of importance and genuine pastoral interest in them

[8] Constitution on the Sacred Liturgy, article 14.

[9] Albert Cardinal Meyer, Chicago, Illinois, March 17, 1961.

will be conveyed to the people, when their priest observes these very basic, and common sense, rules of behavior.

Better still, tape record the sessions. Have them transcribed. Print the salient points in the bulletin.

Group discussion stirs interest in all existing parish organizations. No organization should be slighted. Some groups can very easily make a deeper study of the Mass and participation with great benefit to themselves and the parish—study groups, CFM groups, teenage groups, YCW groups, the Legion of Mary. This, of course, depends on the individual parish.

In particular, the *ushers* are a group of men not to be overlooked. A similar meeting with them can advance the program greatly. Adhere to the basic pattern—group discussion, depersonalization of the regulations, a genuine search for their feelings and suggestions.

It might come as a surprise—often enough, people pitch the ball back to the priest by saying: "Look, Father, just tell us what you want us to do. . . . We'll carry it out." This is a lot different from what might have happened if he had not given them a choice. They have made their choice and ask him, as a religious specialist, to work out the details of the program. That's fine. They are freely accepting it and giving it back to him. They are disposed now to listen. They have "learning-readiness," and the priest is in the position where his effectiveness is highest: *administration as president of the assembly.*

The next step is to call a general meeting of the entire parish for an evaluation of all previous suggestions and discussion. Invite all the people. At this meeting it would be advantageous to have lay people present a synopsis of the conclusions and suggestions of the previous sessions with the choir, ushers and other organizations. Then present the same format used at other meetings for further group discussion and evaluation. Present the regulations from Rome or the chancery, *followed* by an invitation to the people for *free* expression of their feelings and suggestions.

Some will ask questions. Answer them. Again a secretary should take notes, or tape record the entire session.

By Direct Mail?

So far, we have involved only a small number of people. Not too many people will come to a general parish meeting. Not too many people belong to the different parochial organizations anyway, and fewer come to meetings. Somehow we must present the proposition to the people who come to Mass on Sundays but who belong to no parish organization. These can be reached through the Sunday sermon.

These sermons should briefly state the teachings of the church or the regulations from the bishop. They should present a digest of the results of the discussion, suggestions made, the thoughts of different people. Direct quotations of parishioners will convey the image that this is truly a parish project. "Your fellow parishioners said this: . . ." "Another parishioner said that: . . ." Close with the thought, "All of us must feel part of this project *if* we undertake it. Please be free in expressing your opinions, and make your suggestions known concerning the subject of active participation at Mass."

At the same time, we must make an attempt to reach the people who are not in Church—who rarely go to Church—who perhaps come only for Christmas and Easter.

This group can be reached through the mail. The priest should make a report to "all" the parishioners which gives the results of all the meetings. He follows the same general pattern: confront these people with a quotation from the pope, or the regulations from the chancery office. Synopsize the thoughts of the community. Quote those in favor of the program *and* those against it.[11] It might be helpful to quote many

[11] A psychological study of opinion change in *Communication and Persuasion*, by Carl I. Hovland, Irving L. Janis, Harold H. Kelley, states that persuasion and

by name. (Obtain their permission of course. Hardly anyone will object to the use of his name, especially if you quote something that adds to his stature. Use some statements from highly respected parishioners. It will make them enthusiastic promoters of the active participation program.) Finally, he asks the people for their opinions and suggestions. Most people will read a personal letter; only a few will respond in writing. But he has honored all by asking for their suggestions.

The following Sunday, the administration is ready to ask the people for their personal judgment. Thus far we have been allowing them to make self-inquiries, self-explorations concerning participation—the first step of the prudential process. The time now has come for them to take the second step of the process: to make a choice, as it were, to say "Amen" to this participation program. We cannot develop active participation in the parish without this parish approval.

The ushers can distribute mimeographed sheets of paper listing something like the following:

1. When you come to Mass on Christmas, would you like to sing one carol before Mass and one after Mass?__________
2. If your answer is yes, select two carols you would like to sing.

______________________________.______________________________.

(List five or six. Leave one or two lines blank for suggested hymns of their own. Have the ushers collect and tabulate the results.)

All this might seem like much ado about nothing, but it is the first plunge. The beginning step is what is so difficult and

---

communication are more effective in the long run by a two-sided presentation—presentation of both sides of the question—especially with an audience that initially disagrees with the talker's position (New Haven: Yale Univ. Press, 1953) p. 110.

so important. Thus, a small step forward is better than no step at all. A big step threatens, frightens people. This is a small change, true. We should not expect major approval immediately to a full program of participation. On succeeding Sundays, as participation develops, more propositions can be presented.

An alternate approach: After the group discussions among parishioners, the pastor asks parish cooperation in a trial of partial participation, letting them know that at the end of a certain number of weeks, they will be asked for an opinion concerning active participation.

The active involvement of parishioners to this point has consisted of group discussion and group consent. We cannot overstress the importance of these steps: we have honored every parishioner with an invitation to express his opinion, to participate in group discussion; we have honored him with the privilege of making a decision concerning participation; everyone was treated as an adult. Now we should consider the necessity of a deeper active involvement of certain key people.

First of all, the organist.

The organist is one of the most important persons to involve actively. Negative reaction from him can very easily sabotage the entire program. But we cannot expect his enthusiastic support by simply laying the program before him and expecting him to execute it. He must not be treated as a musical puppet—mere executor of the pastor's whim. The subject must be discussed thoroughly with him, asking for his opinions and respecting his suggestions.

This done, the organist will make great sacrifices in cooperating with us in effecting the program. Sometimes priests lament the fact that they know so little about music. This is often an asset, because it forces us to seek information and to rely on professional help, or at least on a person who knows more about music than we do. We can deeply share with him the planning of the program, respecting his opinion, relying on his musical skill. Or, we can simply tell him what we think he should do, what role we want him to play, in the program of introducing participation.

My relationship with two organists illustrates the two approaches. One I took in as co-partner, deeply involving her in the program of participation—the other I simply told what to do and did not actively involve in the program. Later a more active role was extended to the second with immediate results. Perhaps it would be better to let them tell just how they felt, in their own words.

> I felt a leader . . . I felt very much a part of the whole thing. I thought the program was God-centered rather than Father-fashioned. By Father-fashioned I mean this is what Father wants, therefore I *have* to do it because it's my job and Father wants it. We were both working towards the same goal with mutual understanding. You gave me a free hand from the musical standpoint and some of the psychological approach. . . . Really, you made me feel that 98% of the music program was mine.
>
> * * *
>
> I would have strongly resented interference from a non-musician. You could have destroyed my whole enthusiasm had you been more domineering and demanding. . . . Many priests have no respect for our views or opinions as organists. I have heard many organists say they do not really feel a part of the parish program. They are doing only what Father tells them to do. However, once a priest trusts the music program to a musician organist, this is a great confidence. It is a compliment that is very important. It is his trust in you.

The reaction of this second organist came as a shock, really. Having enjoyed such a successful relationship with one organist, one would hardly expect to be such a flop with a second. Yet, I was not aware of any difference of approach at the time. Looking back, I thought I did nothing wrong. All I did was lay out the program in great detail, expecting the second organist to continue where the first one left off.

The second woman is likewise a graduate of a Catholic college. This was her first position. I thought I was being very helpful by pointing out, in detail, what was a success and what was expected, by encouraging progress and improvements in technique, expecting all the while to convey a sense of great importance—a sense of vocation regarding the position. To my surprise, I failed in all things until such time as I stopped giving detailed advice.

This is her side of the story:

> . . . no rapport . . . no communication between us as far as two people working for the same cause. I didn't feel "in" it for a long time until rather recently. . . . You just got under my skin from the beginning. I notice last year you left me on my own a little bit more—you didn't push me. This I appreciated.
>
> For a long time I just felt I wasn't part of it. At first it was just a job. You didn't make me feel a part of the parish or any of its functions. I was just kind of outside. If a person doesn't feel part of what's going on, they are not going to give anything to it.
>
> The attitude of the priest should be one of not telling the organist what to do, but working more or less with her and not talking *down* to her . . . working *with* the organist. Maybe I'm not as competent in all the ways of the former organist—but there must be SOMETHING we could do together if you were interested in this goal. There must be something that I could contribute to it. Even an inferior organist, if she was the poorest example of a musician that has ever come along . . . the worst thing you could ever do is cut her off or let her think she's not of any use around here. If you would include her in on it, she might be inspired to

> greater heights. She might be inspired to go into the subject more deeply if she or he was included as part of it.
>
> . . . You must trust that the person has the ability to do this, rather than tell him this is what *you ought to do.* If you want the maximum results from people, the maximum efforts, I think there is a better way of doing it than you have done.

We can return to such points later, but I think the moral is sufficiently clear: "participation," if we are to use the word with any meaning, begins *before* Mass, and continues on in the life of the parish, all day, every day. The sooner priests and laymen in any parish learn this, the better will the Church be for it.

[2]

With the Men in Mind

We were the key of it. . . . We showed that it isn't the chosen few that are the backbone of the Church. . . . It's the rank and file as we proved here.

A DEEPER active involvement of a large number of men is of immeasurable value to pastor and organist in introducing active participation. First of all, he needs many adult men.

The gathering of a large group of men will not be accomplished without great effort. Nor is it as impossible as it might at first seem—if he lets it be known that it will be of a temporary nature and a cutoff date is given to the men.

The bigger the group, the better—40, 60, 100. The pastor should invite all men of the parish, both young and old, to join this group, including the men of the choir; train them in the hymns of the Mass, with a view to having them introduce the same to the entire parish; deeply share this project with the men; listen even more intently to their suggestions; discuss with them the merits of participation and its problems; convey to them the importance of their responsibility: "You will introduce active participation to the entire parish."

One cannot overstress the value of the leadership of this large group of men responding and singing in the Church. If one started with a children's choir, people are likely to conclude: "Participation is all right for children." If you start with women, the men will say: "It's OK . . . for women. . . ."

Men need men to draw them to participation. The psychological value of this large group of men perched not in a choir loft, but sitting in the Church, in the pews, a part of the congregation, singing and responding, cannot be overemphasized.

Thus the introduction of participation to the entire congregation becomes a cooperative effort between the priest, the organist and these men. We can teach the simple responses and the hymns of the Mass in a variety of ways. Regarding the hymns, the priest can sing the hymn, the people repeat it after him, or the people can repeat it after the organist or a separate leader of song has sung it. But by far the most effective way is for them to listen to the men singing the phrases of the hymn or the response while they, the congregation, repeat it after them.

Similarly regarding the learning of the responses—the priest says, for instance, "Dominus vobiscum," the men answer, "Et cum spiritu tuo." Everyone first listens and then everybody repeats "Et cum spiritu tuo." Let the people hear the group, let the people repeat after the group. The priest is expected to know such things and so is the organist, but people do not expect a large group of men to know it. Hearing the men speaking aloud, and singing the hymns, communicates a sense of confidence, and a *virile* image of active participation which is indispensable.

The men who comprised such a group at St. Rose of Lima were interviewed relative to the role they played. The following comments reflect the spirit of the entire group:

> A terrific inspiration for the parish as a whole.
>
> You just can't get up in front of a group of people in Church and tell them to sing the song. If the Church is full—700-800 people—some will sing, the rest will hem and haw around and not even try. . . . After the congregation heard the men sing, they chimed in with them. . . . We warmed them up and they felt like singing. . . . A guy that drives a truck all day—he's up there singing.

> People think "It must be good. He's no better than I am. If he can do it, so can I."
>
> You have a bunch—50 or 60 men—one guy is a truck driver . . . another guy maybe kills hogs. People just see a bunch of men and of course they say if they can sing, I can too.
>
> It's been proven over and over that people have got to be led. I noticed in Church on Sundays, if I sing and everybody else is quiet around me, pretty soon others around me start to sing. . . . They are going to break out of their self-consciousness. I've heard them.
>
> You notice that they pick up their voices too, because they've got a leader. Everybody is trying to sing, but they are afraid. . . . With the strong background of voices, they all follow.
>
> A group of us together relaxed this parish to the point where they could sing with us and enjoy themselves like we were enjoying ourselves by singing in the front.

The organist evaluated the role of these men thus:

> The men's group was an integral part of our whole program . . . added more volume, more manliness to the tone of singing, strength, power. They gave a stronger background to the whole thing, and inspired the people. Their role was of primary importance. Man is supposed to be leader in any given group. He is head of the house, and he has the same role in the Church. Others will eventually follow him, his household, school children, and the entire congregation at Mass.

It is interesting to note that great numbers of people interviewed, especially men, spoke about being tense, self-conscious, fearful about singing in church, even those who had sung in the choir as children, those who readily sing elsewhere, at home, at the bar. All spoke of the singing of others as drawing them out of their shell. It was not the encouraging talks by the priest that eliminated the psychological block. The strength and power of men's voices calms a congregation and draws it to emulate them. Sharing the responsibility of introducing participation with the 65 men who came to three and four Masses at St. Rose of Lima for a number of Sundays, charged the men with enthusiasm and made them ardent promoters and supporters of active participation. For active participation at Mass, this was actually the spark that was to set the parish afire.

Even so, a fire dies out unless another log is thrown on it. So too, active participation tends to be smothered by an almost inevitable deep-rooted resistance and reaction to change. The log that adds fuel to the fire of participation is the involvement of a group of men as lay commentators. Involving laymen in an active function formerly so restricted to the clergy makes a profound impact upon the congregation.

Lay commentators are the "permanent" group we referred to earlier. Again honor all the men by inviting them to participate as lay commentators. Few, if any, will volunteer. No small effort will be required to recruit and train the group. (These men should be hand-picked for ability. . . .) The interest on the investment of the priest's efforts in training these men will be measured a hundredfold.

As important as the office of lay commentator is from the standpoint of helping the congregation to participate, it carries a much deeper meaning. In the spirit of Vatican II, it symbolizes the true image of the Church, the community of the faithful—the living definition of the Church, priest and people working together. All agree the Church is the community of the faithful, not a personal dynasty of a group of priests or of a pastor. Pius XII referred to the people as the Church: "You are the Church."

So, in the worship of a parish, we must project an accurate image of the "Church" to its community. An exclusive identification of the Church with the clergy is a misleading conception and in practice stultifies the laity. The priest and people are the Church—not either alone, but both together.

One of the finest symbols setting before the people the true reality of the Church is the office of lay commentator. It publicly displays this image of the Church, the priest and people together forming the Church, the parish community. As we worship, so we live and work. Laymen will walk into works of Catholic Action, but only after the clergy, in practice, open the door for them—not just with words of theory and nice talk, but with a weekly invitation, dramatized. Lay commentators help create a living symbol of the Church, the one Mystical Body of Christ.

What to Sing?

Many excellent books and cards for active participation are printed by the Liturgical Press, World Library of Sacred Music, Gregorian Institute and others, but none of these is entirely suitable for use as introductory material. Such material confronts people with many unknown hymns and that, together with the strangeness of such matters as Latin, tends to overwhelm and disorganize. When we begin to learn to play the piano or acquire the art of painting, we begin with practice exercises, something simple, gradually progressing to something more difficult—finally to the most difficult exercises and full involvement of the art.

With this in mind, we strongly suggest that, initially, practice sheets or cards *compiled by the priests of the parish in conjunction with the organist—and whenever possible with the help of other parishioners*, can profitably be used. In this way, one can take into account the language, educational and spiritual backgrounds of the parishioners, their knowledge of hymns and prayers. It is so important to begin with what people already know—and who knows this better than the priest and people of each parish? Each individual is unique—so, obviously, each parish. Participation books for a parish composed mainly of college graduates will differ from that suitable for an Indian or Negro mission, or for an immigrant, foreign language parish.

True, participation must develop within the general framework of the rules set forth by the Constitution on the Sacred Liturgy and other documents of the Church—but not in a necessarily *uniform* way in every parish. What is good for one is not necessarily good for another. For this reason, it is advantageous for each parish to assemble its own material, selecting the hymns and prayers according to its individual needs. Books, cards and hymnals on the market can be looked upon as a smorgasbord from which material may be selected. Publishers will readily grant permission to the parish to reprint the hymns for local use. (Besides, many hymns suitable for introducing participation are public domain.) Modern offset printing, mimeographing or various ditto machines make this possible at a minimum cost.

Participation ought, for that matter, to derive strong nourishment by tapping the roots of our cultural and musical backgrounds, using familiar melodies and hymns. Such hymns provide a valuable psychological substratum; for example, "O Mary, my Mother" strikes a responsive chord for the Germans, "Immaculate Mary" for the French, the wonderful carol "God Supreme" for the Polish. Drawing upon the doctrinally sound, musically virile hymns from Protestant sources is invariably a wise move, which will further create a friendly rapport with those who are not Catholic. Also converts usually treasure the experiences associated with the participated worship of their youth, and familiar melodies help make them achieve a more comfortable psychological and emotional transition to our Catholic way of worship.

One can object that such practice sheets or cards usually look amateurish and perhaps lack technical perfection. This is more than compensated for by other factors. In this way, participation will bear a personal stamp. It becomes the work of "our" pastor, "our" parish, "our" assistant, "our" organist. The work may not be perfect, but it is "ours" and that *is* important.

Perhaps even more important than the "community-stamp" element, this approach provides the atmosphere for original work. It encourages the organist and other musicians to try their hand at composing. It causes them to be more than a little alert for new material and to find ways to improve participation. It gives the priests more than a checkbook responsibility toward participation material. It is good for the priest and organist to feel such mutual responsibility which carries its own rewards—a sense of accomplishment and a built-in enthusiasm builder—values hardly to be ignored. Such participation tends to become more living, less stereotyped. It is not taken for granted, but becomes the focus of everyone's attention.

One must be careful not to substitute a straitjacket of external participation for a straitjacket of silence. Constructive changes in living worship will not be so much the fruit of brilliant minds working in the cells of monasteries, as they will arise out of the alert evaluation of changes made in the laboratories of parish worship. When a priest forces himself to compile participation material, he places himself in this atmosphere—in a laboratory studying towards a new liturgy for our times. He turns the searchlight of his reason and experience on ways to improve community worship.

Where to Start

Some parishes have introduced active participation at the monthly communion Sunday of the Holy Name Society, or the National Council of Catholic Women. Others began with the children, at the children's Mass. Still others selected one or another Mass on Sunday. But permit us to say it again: whatever is done ought to be done by the parish as a whole. A small step into participation *by the entire parish* is more valuable than a gigantic step by one of the parish organizations, or at a particular Mass on Sunday.

If participation is introduced only at the children's Mass, many adults automatically tag it "for children only." Introduction at the monthly Mass of an organization can give the impression that participation is a prize possession of this closed corporation. Introducing it at only one of the Sunday Masses sets up a climate for criticism, and it can often surround the project with the drastic aura of passing novelty.[1]

Anyway, one *ought* to think of worship in terms of the entire parish rather than in a segmented way. We think of parish finances in parish terms. We don't customarily consider what this organization contributes, or what the children contribute. So ought we to look at active participation and its introduction on a parish-wide basis. When introduced, it should be introduced at all the (Sunday) Masses.

The simple Latin responses are often suggested as the first step into participation. However, when we considered our community as a whole, and not just select groups of them, we found that Latin was an unknown language—and congregational participation at Sunday Mass was an unknown experience. I suggest that these basic experiences are *not* unique.

Easy as they seem to learn, even the simple Latin-responses pose a threat to most laypeople. Beginning with a language familiar to them puts them more at ease, because it makes them less fearful. Thus, a favorable, that is, uniformly favorable, reaction should not be expected if the Latin responses are the

[1] Since the attendance at certain Masses may be in a constant state of flux—new members moving into the parish, people coming to the Mass occasionally—these with their spirit of unacquaintance, or disinterest, all more than likely unprepared for participation, can smother it.

initial step into active participation. Both positive and negative feelings are aroused. Prayer habits are disturbed in both priest and people. Enthusiastic response is consequently lacking, and only with great effort will participation be kept alive.

Typical comments are, "Well, saying the Latin is strange," or, "I suppose I'll get used to it." We must accept a basic fact here: the Roman rite, even with the considerable reforms enacted by the Council, is *bi*-lingual. Some of the Latin responses in one form or another will remain for quite a while. Thus, for the people Latin can easily become a sort of burden, rather than a free and intelligent expression of our inner being. It falls into the category of "something we *have* to do," and not "something we want to do."

When to Start

When to start? As scientists look for a favorable climate to launch a rocket shot, we must look for the proper human climate for the shot into active participation. No better psychological moment can be found in our day than Christmas. People are brimming with the spirit of generosity, bursting to sing carols when given the opportunity. Besides, it's the day the greatest number of parishioners are present at Mass. So it is that the initial proposal to the people becomes the singing of a carol before and after Mass on Christmas.

A choice must be made here between the spoken and the sung prayer. We selected the sung prayer because by its very nature music disciplines more than does speech. The rhythm and time value of every note gently forces a group to do something in unison. Perhaps no songs are better known or more enjoyed by all people than the Christmas carols. Few have experienced singing these familiar carols as a congregation in Church. Thus we introduce them to the new experience of congregational singing with a key that is already in the possession of everyone, which brings out what they already know, and which, perhaps, is just letting them do what they always wanted to do.

It was a little amusing for me to find that people who strongly objected to participation in Church readily accepted congregational carol singing. A group objecting to participation was so violently opposed that I posed the question to them: "Now when Christmas comes, let us say we have no more singing of carols at Christmas Mass." The entire group thundered a chorus of "no's."

Then too, stepping into participation with carols does not pose a major threat to any pastor or priest. Few priests find it easy to adapt themselves to participation. We are strapped to routine far more than we care to admit, and even priests ordained only a few years will find adjusting to active participation rather difficult, if not unnerving. Full active participation, for example, demands considerable changes in one's pace, and especially in the loudness of the voice. None of the many small adaptations will come easily. Carol singing makes the first step easier for everybody, because it takes a minimum of effort.

But with these additions, for the first time, *every* Catholic in the parish has had a chance to experience the joy of active participation. No one's prayer habits are disturbed, neither the priest who is "offering" the Mass, nor the participating people. One hymn sung by the entire parish benefits the parish more than if a few individuals reached a higher degree of participation at one of the Sunday Masses. Positive feelings toward participation are awakened. Priests have an experiential awareness that the people *can* sing in Church and *enjoy* doing it as a congregation. We can readily imagine that the congregation comments favorably within the family circles of the parish about singing carols in Church. And this degree of enthusiastic response will go a long, long way in building up the priest's morale—and not only for participation.

Initial success brings the satisfaction that encourages priest and people to reach out for further achievements in participation. The kindled flame is kept alive and fanned to burn more brightly by periodically presenting propositions which the congregation will readily accept. "We sang so well on Christmas, let us try to keep the Christmas spirit alive for the Sunday after Christmas by singing the same carols." Then: "Since everyone enjoyed singing the Christmas carols so much, how about trying, for the next four Sundays to sing, 'Holy God' at the end of Mass, after the priest's blessing?" "The response has been so good, we thought we might want to begin next Sunday's Mass by singing one verse of 'Come Holy Ghost.' Let's experiment with this for the next four Sundays."

Such propositions need not be put down in writing and be given to the people for a written assent to each and every one, but the priest must present them in such a way as to let people know they have a choice.

To the priest who is directing the project at this point, we suggest that after a few months of singing hymns with which they are acquainted, having introduced a hymn at the Offertory, you may ask the people if they have enjoyed the singing of the hymns thus far and if they care to begin saying an English prayer—for example, the Gloria to express, as a community, praise to God—or the Nicene Creed as a public expression of Faith—or for that matter, any "English prayer approved by competent territorial bodies of bishops legitimately established." [2]

Visualize here the emergence of participation on a *parochial* basis, moving slowly, continuously from what people know to what they do not know—from known English hymns to an unknown English hymn, then to spoken English prayers. After the community is at ease participating, singing and speaking aloud in the English language, we introduce them to one Latin response. (Yes, one Latin response at a time.) Finally, to the

[2] Constitution on the Sacred Liturgy, Vatican II, p. 22, #2.

"Agnus Dei" sung in measured music, to the "Agnus Dei" sung in Gregorian Chant, allowing time intervals between each step.[3] Some parishioners will want to sprint ahead in active participation. The entire parish should progress together, slowly if necessary, and steadily. Periodically the priest may present different propositions to the people.

All this is a psychological and mechanical skeleton for introducing active participation. Every parish will have to clothe it with flesh, each in its own way, to make it living. For the priest, as far as the presentation of propositions to the people is concerned—how frequently or what kind, the choice of hymns, the old hymn, the new hymn, at what pace they are introduced, introduction of each prayer, type of prayer, introduction of responses, singing of the Ordinary of the Mass—all of this no one can tell you how to do. Each must learn in his own way, on his own responsibility, at his own pace. In this way, the priest, as shepherd of his people, takes hold of the mantle of leadership of active participation in the liturgy in his parish and more fully accepts the responsibility for parish worship.

[3] In this chapter, as in other chapters, some may say this particular point has no relevance, but in the light of the opening of the door to the vernacular in the Mass, it may be worth bearing in mind the Constitution on the Sacred Liturgy, p. 36, #1, "Particular law remaining in force, the use of the Latin language is to be preserved in the Latin rites"; and p. 54, ". . . Nevertheless steps should be taken so that the faithful may also be able to say or to sing together in Latin those parts of the Ordinary of the Mass which pertain to them." So we must certainly take into consideration the introduction of *some* Latin to the people, regardless of how much vernacular has been introduced into the Mass by legitimately constituted groups of bishops. This applies both to recited and High Masses. It seems to me that both languages might be used, indiscriminately, depending on the musical setting.

[3]

All This Talking in Church

I am bothered and don't like it. In fact I stopped coming here.

A COMPLIMENT gladdens the heart, and priests are no exception. Opposition causes everyone concern. Statements such as the following will encourage everyone to be an ardent promoter and supporter of active participation:

> Before if I missed Mass on a Sunday, so what? It was nothing. But since they started the recited Mass as we have it here, I feel I am a part of the Mass. I don't miss Mass. I wouldn't think of it. It wouldn't be Sunday without Mass. It's something I look forward to every week. Instead of it being a duty, it has become a privilege.

> I wasn't from this parish. It was quite by accident that I came one Sunday. It was all so new to me, belonging to a different parish as I did. We didn't have the recited Mass at all. It was so welcome—so good to be able to express yourself with everyone. I continued to come. I just couldn't have it any other way now.

And the most staunch supporter of active participation will be shaken a bit by a remark such as:

> I don't enjoy going to Church because we have to participate. I don't like to go to St. Rose's any more.

How should the priest react to those who resist participation, who openly object to it, who display hostility? This can hurt, but the ointment that soothes the wounds is the kind acceptance and sincere understanding of people who react in opposition. Simply to understand them calms their feelings. We must bear each other's burdens. The whole introduction and development of a participation program must be saturated with understanding.

A priest, then, must step down from the pulpit and into the pews—take off his collar and put on a tie and take a look at participation through the eyes, mind and heart of the parishioner. He must understand the struggles of parishioners with participation; and for some, it is a rending struggle. He must struggle *with* them as they adjust to this new manner of worship. He must seek to understand their prayer habits, their feelings, their attitudes, their emotional reactions to change, their attitude toward Latin, toward singing, toward participation in general, becoming aware of the emotionally charged atmosphere—their hostility to him, manifested subtly in one form or another. No amount of enthusiasm, no amount of persuasion, encouragement or psychological help on the part of the priest will substitute for a sincere understanding of his parishioners. A direct assault rarely, if ever, helps. Rather, let him publicly express his understanding of them and thus communicate to them that he sympathizes with their self-consciousness, their embarrassment, their disturbances. Priests must take this as a general rule: we must understand, and *express* our understanding and honest sympathy, with our fellow-parishioners as they struggle to make active participation part and parcel of their Sunday worship, as they wrestle with new regulations, as they make new and radical adjustments in their prayer life.

Why Change?

We have been doing it this same way for all these years, and now we have to change? How come?

That plea will be fairly typical, and it will be honest. Yet, each parishioner reacts uniquely to participation. There are no two alike. Among some, there is an apparent similarity in reaction, but even in this there is a difference. The reaction of some is unusually strange—hard to believe. A priest will find it very helpful if he asks his parishioners how they feel towards participation once it has been introduced.

Many express a deep disturbance and irritation at the interference of active participation with their personal prayer and their personal purpose in going to Church. These excerpts of interviews may be helpful in understanding how parishioners really feel, and what they are going through at the time.

> After I heard it the first time, I came outside and I said: Uh-*uh*, this won't do! I just came here to tell my troubles. I figured I would say my prayers and then watch the priest, but oh, all this going on. Can't get used to it.
>
> I go equipped. I have my Rosary and my prayerbook; but I always have that feeling "Here comes the confusion." Somehow I don't get the things done that I came for. The quiet Mass was nice. I could concentrate on the things that happened to me during the week that I liked and didn't like and I could still get the Rosary in.
>
> The recited Mass interrupts your thoughts, your concentration on the Mass and your prayers. Many times I walk in with the intention of praying. I start to pray and I offer my Mass for the deceased, and so on. Out of the clear sky I am interrupted. I forget about everything.
>
> They talk and sing and I forget what I want to say. I want to concentrate on something and I can't because I hear all those other noises—the singing and everything.
>
> I was disturbed when I felt I should have been praying. I was worried about it.

When people view participation as an obstacle to their

prayer, a variety of hostile emotions are aroused and expressed. Participation takes on the form of an attack. People become defensive and hostile and either withdraw more deeply into a shell of personal prayer or openly "attack" the priest.

> I decided to keep on doing what I was doing. To tell the truth, I try not to pay any attention to you.
>
> I distinctly tried to bury my head in the Missal.
>
> When you first started all this rigamarole about singing out loud and about participation, I thought you were nuts.

Others elaborated on their resistance to change:

> You can't break away from the old ways just like that. It's hard to break away from it. When you participate in the regular Mass like I have for about thirty years and a change comes in like that, you begin to wonder "What *is* this?" This is just like taking a bunch of people, setting them down in the benches and telling them to all at once say their Confession publicly.

Statements like these cause one to wonder whether resistance to change was due to the change itself, or rather because the changes were made without sufficient explanation. A child will follow a simple order, but an adult looks for the effect and demands an explanation. A change without explanation is a form of attack, causing people to become defensive and hostile. This points to the need of a more rational, prudential approach to introducing participation, as well as other things. The presentations of reasons for change are of utmost importance. It has been proven sufficiently that resistance to change lessens when reasons are given for such a change. Emotional reaction changes when reason places before us a different picture. A person views "change without reason" one way and "change with the following reasons" another way. Thus, a great deal of hostility toward participation frequently is due to a faulty presentation. When people understand for themselves, opposition lessens.

One cannot unequivocably say that the chief opposition to participation comes from attachment to personal prayer or resistance to change. That these were present in our parish we cannot deny. However, the ratio was not as great as one would believe.

Attachment to personal prayer is relaxed and resistance dislodged by a realistic, experiential knowledge of the structure of the Mass. Until this experiential knowledge takes hold, many people are wholly lacking in the knowledge that participation—singing—is praying. Complete failure in introducing participation oftentimes is more the result of imposition of it on the people rather than setting the foundation through the prudential process in the parishioners. No amount of knowledge, of course, will dislodge all resistance. A need to understand the reaction and not oppose it is of utmost importance.

A Word About Latin

> Learning the Latin responses held us back because we didn't know how to pronounce the words and we were afraid.

By far the biggest obstacle to participation encountered in St. Rose's was extreme difficulty in coping with the Latin.[1] Again, it is important to understand the struggle of the parishioners with the Latin—this was a definite obstacle to our participation. In addition, preoccupation with Latin pronuncia-

[1] Since the Constitution on the Sacred Liturgy states that steps should be taken so that the faithful may also be able to say or to sing together in Latin those parts of the Ordinary of the Mass which pertain to them (par. 54), the insights of the people regarding the Latin are significant and it is very helpful to be aware of them.

tion becomes a detriment to prayerfulness. Fear of making a mistake causes real emotional blocks within many people. Express sympathy with them in their struggles. *Don't* tell them it's easy. The truth is it is extremely difficult for them. Some never master it.

> I try to pronounce the words and never get finished. I get tongue-tied in the middle and I stop dead.
>
> I get so nervous. I don't even know how to get the words out. I just can't keep up.[2]
>
> I feel embarrassed. They are our prayers and I can't say them in Latin. I say "O God, come on help me with this." I'm afraid to pronounce the words wrong. That's why I keep quiet.
>
> I can't get to first base with it. After the first line, I'm stuck.
>
> The words get all mixed up and are ineffective because you don't know what you are saying.
>
> I don't feel like I'm praying in Church when I respond in Latin. I'm just trying hard to pronounce all the words and that's all it is to me. I don't know what I'm saying in the first place.
>
> People are hesitant to speak out when they can't pronounce the words. They feel kind of foolish and you really do. When you mispronounce the Latin word, you feel kind of silly and then you keep quiet.
>
> It's confusing. You say a bunch of words that you have learned to repeat and that's all.

Parallel quotations were voiced by both young and old, men and women. Can anyone blame them for resistance to change? Can anyone blame them for wanting to cling to personal

[2] Our pace is slow, with many pauses, sometimes to the point where we almost drag. So this is not the speed of the priest.

prayer—one was prayer, the other not? People were more expressive and voiced opposition more strongly to the Latin than to interference with private prayer or change. Apparently it is very frustrating and discouraging not to be able to pronounce the Latin words. But most important of all, to people who do not understand it, praying in Latin does not seem to be praying.

Self-Consciousness

> I feel very much ill at ease. It seems like everybody is looking at me and throwing daggers.

Active participation poses a definite threat to many people. The presence of a threat arouses the emotion of fear. The emotion of fear, coupled with self-consciousness, has been expressed as a dominant obstacle to participation. People also felt threatened by the presence of one another, even though these be their own family members. They became very self-conscious of people sitting next to them. As chief obstacles to participation, fear and self-consciousness seem to follow closely behind people's difficulty with the Latin.

> That's why I don't like to go to church with my wife. She sits next to me and when I start singing, she starts and makes me stop all of a sudden. She looks at me and kind of snickers. I can tell she is laughing at me.

> I felt self-conscious when I first walked in and saw those papers in the pew and everybody picked them up and sang. I just didn't feel like I was at home. It was altogether new and I just didn't feel like letting out. I thought it was probably silly or something.

> The whole thing is fear. It's fear.

> I didn't want to sing. I just wanted to forget it. A lot of people can't sing very well and they are conscious of it. I

> thought "These people, they might hear me sing. I'm not going to sing," and so I just sit there and watch. I'm afraid to say anything because I know the person in front of me. If he hears me singing, he might think I'm an idiot, so I sit quiet so he won't hear me.
>
> I'd never sing in church. My voice carries and I'd be the only guy up there with a deep voice and everybody'd turn around and look at me. You're self-conscious, you know, and most of the people in the church are—they're self-conscious too. Everybody is scared of making a mistake. Everybody'll look at them.
>
> When I sit alongside my daughter, I feel so embarrassed. She can answer every prayer. I can't catch up at all. I try to—so hard—and can't. I'm so afraid somebody else will hear me say wrong words.
>
> At first it seemed you were careful who you were next to. You didn't want to answer because you might not know how to pronounce the words or sing them, so you kept still. As it went on, you got used to it.
>
> I won't go to church with my kids because they laugh at me. One time I had the boys with me and I started to sing. They thought it was the biggest joke and I told them I would never go to Mass with them again.

Very many, men in particular, were in the grips of self-consciousness and fear—ever present factors that keep them from fuller participation. Kindness and understanding settle these emotions. Having a large group of men singing as a group in the congregation has much emphatic value. (This is how we came to understand the need).

Others expressed related feelings such as embarrassment, strangeness and confusion.

> It was very strange. It was unusual. I was embarrassed. I didn't know exactly what to do, not being aware of

> when to stand or when to respond to the different parts. I had this feeling of just being lost.
>
> I thought I was in the wrong church. It seemed strange to me. I didn't know if I was even in a Catholic church. When I came out, I looked to see what church I was in.
>
> I felt I was doing the wrong thing in the right place.

I could hardly believe the reactions of some, so strange were they to me. Often people restated, with great seriousness, their obstacles and were surprised that I didn't readily accept them. These obstacles were most real to them. Other emotional reactions that were equally deep-rooted were expressed, too, but these were not so common.

> I felt kind of strange because I thought it was supposed to be a place of all silence where everybody stood and watched.

At times, virtues acquired in childhood become a stumbling block in adulthood. Emphasis on training to be silent in church proved a major stumbling block for many.

> It hit me awfully hard, talking out. I didn't think it was right. We were trained not to talk in church. I thought it was terrible.
>
> I never felt right at first, talking out loud when we were supposed to be quiet. I never liked that. I felt like I was in a movie lobby. I couldn't understand this talking out loud in church when we were taught to be quiet. I thought it was wrong.
>
> When they first started the recited Mass, I'll bet half the parish felt the same as I: "What are they, a bunch of nuts, talking in church like that?"

To some, participation brought back association with past unpleasant memories—stereotyped reactions, as for example:

> I go to church to pray. If I had to go to church with the

> thought "It's like going to school, that I have to answer questions in Latin," I cannot feel I am in church.
>
> When I was single and shortly after I first got married, I went to church with my mother. We did quite a lot of singing. This kind of brings back the memory of my mother's death and I just don't care for it any more. I used to enjoy it with Ma.

People rarely *express* such stereotyped, conditioned reactions, but they are more common than we would suspect or care to believe.

Others felt they were taking on a responsibility that didn't belong to them.

> I felt as though we were interfering with the altar boys, because all the years I've been going to Mass, the people were always quiet and it was just the altar boys that answered the priest. I felt I shouldn't be doing this. It was something more of an honor for the altar boys. We were just supposed to be onlookers.
>
> All we are doing by participating is taking away from the priest.
>
> By having the Mass as we are having it now, we are placing ourselves, I think, on the same level with the priests.

A negligible number objected to the singing—again perhaps from failure to recognize that song is prayer or by reason of lack of singing ability.

> I go to church to pray, not to sing. I just don't feel right when I'm in church—you go to start saying the Rosary and then they tell you to turn the page to so and so and sing. To me, I don't go there to sing. I'm not a singer and I don't intend to ever be one.

Against the background of the following once rather common conception of a priest, some people felt unworthy to participate.

> My father always said the priest was God. I'm 48 years old and I've been brought up with the knowledge that when the priest shook his finger, I shook. He was God. Participation belongs more to the Religious Orders. I live a different life compared to the priests and nuns. I don't think I'm worthy to participate. How many people in the state of mortal sin come in church and pick up the leaflets and start reading them and saying the Mass? I don't think that's right. It loses the important atmosphere. I always felt the Mass was strictly for the priest.

Lack of knowledge of what was taking place disturbed many people, who expressed their chagrin more forcefully.

> The first time they had it and they passed out the booklets, everybody stood there kind of surprised—"What's this?"

> Well, I'll tell the truth, Father, I'm not going behind the bush at all. I thought: "What is this Father John thinking about?" I couldn't understand why you were trying to change things, especially for us old people who don't understand one word about it. "What's he going to do next?" I used to say that every Sunday—and then when Father Fearon started . . . goodbye!

> I know so many people said the same thing—at first they were very irritated because they didn't know what was going on.

One or two preferred to follow the Mass more meditatively.

> I like to stop and meditate. At different times, different prayers mean more to you. You might spend more time on certain prayers than you would on others, depending on how you feel at the time, whereas in the recited Mass, you just have to keep on moving. It just seems as though I don't get anything out of it.

To others, participation seemed like an empty reading exercise without meaning.

> I'm just reading prayers . . . reading a lot of words and not really getting anything out of it. I'm doing it only from habit, just like anything else—from habit, and I don't like it.

It is interesting to note that some began to get irritated with the *non*-participants. With such reaction a priest might be pleased, but it can backfire. A too-open irritation on the part of a participant toward those who do not participate is a threat. It can cause them to become more adamant in their obstinacy rather than help win the others over.

> If I look around and see someone who isn't singing, it irritates me. I feel like telling them to pick up the sheets and participate.

> The only distraction I find is that everyone doesn't take up the hymn card. That is distracting to me.

Surely these excerpts do not exhaust the reactions of our people to participation, nor do they necessarily express their deepest feelings and attitudes. Human reactions are more complex than these quotations indicate, but this sampling does open a new view of parishioner's feelings, thus enabling us—laity and clergy—to better cope with the human difficulties in participation. (The study will be even more worthwhile if it inspires priests to find out for themselves, by questioning their parishioners on THEIR reactions.)

Finally, many other parallel obstacles exist that we could not unearth in our interviews. Some of the obstacles expressed were, and are, very deeply rooted. Hearing them aroused my sympathy. It was a plea from our people for my patience and understanding:

Understand us, give us time; and we will work out our difficulties and become enthusiastic participants. . . .

[4]

Sympathy and Leadership

GENERALLY we resent regulations if they are contrary to our past habits of acting or thinking. As we are carrying out the regulations, the pressure of contrary feelings and emotions can and usually does increase. This is especially true in the Church, if we do not see the reasonableness of the new rules, or (most often) when we have a highly developed sense of good, old pride. Pressure of adverse emotions can hold us back from carrying out the regulations when introducing active participation. That priests should meet with opposition from parishioners surely should not come as a surprise. It is quite understandably human, particularly as regards participation. Opposition here stems not from the lack of intellectual understanding of what active participation is, nor from the lack of knowledge of the technique, so much as from emotional blocks—the chief obstacles to participation. A parish must relax the grip of these emotions, loose their tightness, help bring them into reasonable balance.

A priest can begin this by providing opportunities for people to release negative feelings and emotions. Just to talk about pent-up feelings helps. If we are understood as we speak about our negative feelings, they are mitigated all the more. Thus, it is most advantageous to provide an occasion for people to release negative feelings. People may air their gripes personally to the priest, or group gatherings can be set up for such release. One might very well enlist a group of people who would go through the parish, asking for opinions, letting people blow off steam. Telephoning parishioners is another helpful way of obtaining information and diminishing some of the negative reactions. Personal approach to key people in the parish is advisable. Converts to participation become ardent supporters. Encourage people to talk about participation in their family gatherings, among their friends. Certainly—since it is not possible for all parishioners to air their emotions to the priest personally—let them air them to one another. Just to hear what other parishioners think has been tremendously helpful to many people.

Again: A public recognition of the negative feelings of the community is equally important. No, it is not enough to give an intellectual explanation of the theology of participation or the theology of the Mystical Body, although these are vital in their proper place. Nor is it sufficient to train the congregation in the techniques of Latin or English pronunciation, in the recited prayers, in learning to sing, and so forth.

All these things are necessary. But more than these, at this stage of the project a priest should offer a sermon—or two, or three, or as many as seem necessary—which recognizes the difficulties at hand. Understanding must become the foundation of every such instruction on participation.

I gave the following talk in an attempt to make clear that, as their priest, I understood some of the difficulties our people were experiencing, as well as some of their positive reactions:

> The Church wants us to begin active participation. This is in conformity with its regulations. But we're all human. Many of us will dislike it. Some of us will be deeply disturbed. It just isn't going to be easy. Together we are going to have to work this out.
>
> No, it isn't going to be easy to slip the Rosary back into our pocket or put down the prayerbook we have been using for thirty, forty, fifty years. It isn't going to be easy to interrupt the reading of our Missal to sing a hymn. It isn't going to be easy to lay aside our personal prayers to pray the Mass.
>
> We know this is the mind of the Church. We realize

that like anything else, it's one thing to know what we ought to do—but it is another thing to do it. It's very understandable that some of us will resent the changes. Let's see if we can untangle our problems and lessen our resentments.

Learning the Latin surely won't be easy. There may be some of us here to whom it will be no problem at all, but for many of us it's going to be difficult to learn to pronounce even a few strange words. It isn't going to be easy to learn the words whether you are sixty years old or forty, or a convert who has never heard them before he entered the Catholic Church. It's hard to pronounce foreign words or to say something we really don't understand. Some of us may be embarrassed to pronounce the words. Others will get tongue-tied, mixed up. Most of us who have never learned Latin probably will be saying: "Why do we have to do this?" "Why did they ask us to say the Latin?"

These difficulties are very understandable. Many of the things we are going to say almost seem to have no meaning. We may even say: "It doesn't seem like we're even praying. The words are so difficult, we get behind so fast." This is all part of our struggle. We'll all be struggling with these and the many other things to make our worship the worship the Church desires.

When we haven't sung for years in Church and never prayed out loud regularly, we can really become self-conscious. We're afraid to say something out loud because somebody might hear it—especially if we're not sure how to pronounce the words. We're afraid of making a mistake. We look to see who is in front of us, behind us; cast a glance to the right and to the left. This is an awful feeling—this feeling of self-consciousness. It can hold us back from really giving ourselves fully to God. Some of us may say, "Seems like everybody is looking at me." We are afraid to let out our voices—especially if we have a deep voice.

Most of us really want to participate. We want to learn how to do it. We want to learn to sing, to pray together, but ever present is that fear.

It isn't going to be easy to break out of our self-consciousness. It's real—this self-consciousness, this fear of our neighbor. Even if the one who is sitting next to us is our husband or our wife or our own children, we're just afraid that they might snicker at us if we sing off key, or they might laugh at us or make some remark when we get home. Both you and I will be struggling through these difficulties.

It might even strike us rather strangely when all of a sudden everybody is praying out loud. Oh, we've said Hail Mary's in Church and maybe a few other prayers, but during the whole Mass? To hear a lay commentator? A *layman* read the Sacred Scriptures? This surely is strange. It's hard to get used to.

We might even feel that we are taking over the altar boy's job. We might feel it's his job to answer the priest, and here we are taking his part. We might wonder why it was good enough to have the altar boys answer for so many years, so why not let it continue that way.

It is very understandable that we might find it hard —that we might resent it—that we might be afraid and self-conscious as we begin active participation. But we have done other things in the past that haven't been easy and we'll work this out, too. For a while we expect some not to cooperate and we won't feel hurt. We'll try to be patient. You might even be saying, "Father, you're making it sound worse than it really will be." Then again you may say, "Father, be patient with us, take it easy with us and we'll work this out together."

Some of us may already be saying, "We really enjoy going to Church now." "We appreciate the Mass to a far greater extent than ever before." Some might even find the Mass boring without participation—that it drags. Participation does seem to make the Mass go

> faster, at least for *some* of us. It really is satisfying to gain a deeper understanding of the Mass. Participation makes us feel more a part of the Mass. It's easier for some of us to stay awake. We can really feel at home at times—like all the people belong together, like everybody's a family when we are participating.
>
> As hard as it is to accept participation and as self-conscious as we may be, yet, at the same time, participation does seem to give a feeling of togetherness—that we are a family parish, praying and singing together, as we offer the Sacrifice of the Mass.

This talk was given one evening to a group of parishioners for their reactions. Some felt people ought to be exposed to participation first for one week, then such a talk given. Others thought that the talk should be given before and after participation has been introduced. After a brief discussion, it was generally agreed that it would be advantageous to give this talk before and after participation has been begun. The following comment perhaps synopsizes the attitude of the people:

> If we had this talk given to us instead of having a priest going up and down the aisle telling us to pick up our booklets and to sing, participation would have been easier to accept.

Because a sizeable number of people are not in church on any given Sunday, it is good, from time to time, to make an announcement aimed at removing emotional blocks. Instead of covering a gamut of feelings, one feeling, developed briefly, can convey understanding in a few short sentences. We suggest the following pattern:

1. Take a feeling known to be an obstacle to participation.
2. Activate this feeling by speaking in general terms about the feeling, recalling a parallel incident in life. Avoid speaking specifically.

3. Recall the pleasant outcome.
4. Draw a parallel in regard to active participation. Speak slowly and deliberately.

For example, the confusion people now feel at Mass. Recall the experience of being lost, confused; the pleasant relief as one untangles the confusion and finds the way home. Draw the parallel to active participation:

> I'm sure all of us have experienced, at some time in our lives, the feeling of being lost—perhaps as children, even as adults. How disturbing it was especially in a strange territory. It's so confusing—not knowing where to go—and so upsetting.
>
> It's such a tremendous relief to find the way home. It's relieving, relaxing, so good to be home, to be again in a safe place, secure.
>
> It's all too easy to get lost following the new Mass: so confusing doing things in a new, different way. It's upsetting, not knowing what is going on. It feels good to find the way *home* after being lost. We can look forward with relief to feeling at home again with the Mass. We *will* feel relaxed again, participating at Mass in the new way, but it may take a little time.

Or a short talk relative to the difficulty of making a change:

> In our lives, we find it hard to make changes. I'm sure we have experienced the difficulty of taking a chance—change of job, change of residence. We will recall once we have to make a change we begin to feel insecure—anxious—because with the old way, we were so much at ease. It can be a very lonely feeling all of a sudden, just before we make the change, as we wonder: "Am I doing the right thing?" It's awfully hard to break away from a set pattern. We are afraid to make a change. It will get anybody all tensed up. It's the unknown that kills us. I guess this is why we resist change so much. Yet, as we look back over our lives, when we did make a change, perhaps to a new job or to a new way of doing things, we

were satisfied and pleased; we felt settled and content. I suppose in the same way we are afraid to make a change following the Mass in a different way. We feel secure with the old.

Yet when we do make a change, we're quite happy with it. I suppose in time many of us will feel quite happy and secure in the new way of participating at Mass. That's the way things normally work out for us. We resist change, feel very insecure about making it, yet once we do it we're quite happy. We feel quite satisfied. We've accomplished something. It's a challenge when we overcome something so hard, but we really have a sense of achievement afterwards.

A talk on the emotion of fear as an obstacle to participation:

As we look back into our lives, we recall many occasions when we have been afraid. When you stop to think, we still are afraid of many things. Fears are real, very real. They cripple us, paralyze us to the point of holding us back from doing a lot of things that we want to do. Giving in to fear leads to a real letdown. Failure makes us feel like we want to crawl underneath some place and hide. Hardly anything we can do about it: when the pounding heart wins out, it makes us feel like two cents. It leaves us with a feeling of guilt, a lot of dissatisfaction. But when we overcome fear, it's so rewarding, so satisfying and so relaxing. The whole body feels loose, as if everything broke loose, as if the wires tying us together broke loose. We feel if we can conquer this, then we can conquer that, too. We can climb the next mountain. Success really inspires us to do more, to feel really courageous. I'm sure that here in this church, many of us are a little bit afraid—to speak out! We're afraid to make another mistake, afraid to sing out; though, when you stop to think, it would really be rewarding, wouldn't it, if we did overcome this fear? It would be really satisfying—if we overcame the fear and sang! And answered our priest! It's one of those strange facts of being human, that when we're afraid, and we give in to the fear, we feel in a way childish. But it will feel good to overcome fear. It will feel good to conquer this fear especially in church, because this is our Father's house.

Here is a brief talk discussing the difficulties of self-consciousness:

I don't suppose that there is anyone in church who has not sometime in the past felt self-conscious—at work, or at home, among friends, at school. We tighten up inside, afraid to make the wrong move, afraid we're going to say the wrong thing, afraid we're not going to be able to use the right words. We freeze up, and end up keeping quiet. We just can't seem to pull ourselves together. When we overcome or win out over our self-consciousness, it fills us with elation, and inspires us to try more. Success is so sweet; it makes us feel courageous, and brave—we can do just about anything. Sure, many of us here are self-conscious—about saying the responses or about singing out loud. But it's good to look forward to the feeling of success in singing with ease, in saying the prayers with confidence—and all in a very relaxed manner. Even now many people are enjoying participating in the Mass, and feel very much relaxed. Many of us feel like we could just do about anything. It's nice to look forward to it, the feeling of success. The sooner we all try, together, the sooner we will *be* a success.

Some examples of spot announcements:

1. We are going to sing the hymn *Praise to the Lord*, on page 10. It may be hard to put away your Rosary. Please feel free to sing with us.

2. Some of us might be too ashamed even to try to say the prayers. You may pray the Gloria with us as we join the priest.

3. We may feel a little self-conscious about singing. It may seem like everybody is looking at us or throwing daggers at us. Please join us in singing the Offertory hymn on page 51.

4. When we like to follow the Mass with a Missal, it is hard to lay it aside for a while. Please join in singing the Offertory hymn which you will find on page 114.

5. It may seem a little strange to answer the responses that the altar boys always have answered, but you may make the responses for the Preface which can be found on page 25.

These few examples of the short spot announcements which should be made quite frequently, especially in the beginning, could be multiplied greatly. People are very appreciative of an understanding approach, rather than the direct-command method: "Turn to page so and so and SING; turn to page so and so and ANSWER THE PRIEST!" One must, of course, be constantly aware of the emotional tone, the depth of emotional struggle which the members of a parish experience with participated liturgy. The reasons are too numerous to list, but one cogent factor is that over a period of time, the problems of a liturgical program *change*. These spot commentaries, therefore, should be freely adapted, as much as, and whenever, necessary.

Again, it's very important for a priest to know how his parishioners are thinking, what they are feeling and why. The closer the priest and the team of commentators come to expressing what the congregation really thinks and feels, the better off the parish worship program will be. Nobody should be so presumptuous as to *guess:* we must really know our people, we who are to lead. (The discussion of Negative Reactions to Participation can serve as a guide.)

Personal experience here is the best teacher. The entire Mass team must experience the emotions of the congregation, see it, hear it for themselves. All of them should approach the parishioners and sincerely ask them how they feel about the program—not on just one occasion, by any means. They must be constantly alert for changes in the emotional tone. This is a very practical point, and one which can be easily dismissed or rationalized away. On the part of those who are to serve, it demands a sense of humor, which is the most delicate form of the virtue of humility. But in any case, it *must* be done. And it's well worth the lessons it will teach those who must do the asking. As a priest, I testify to my own growth because the people were so honest, and so generous, as to tell me about myself.

[5]

The Liturgy Teaches

Unless we know what the Mass really is, what good is participation?

WITH one voice, our parish expressed the desire to understand the Mass more. All agreed that the explanations that were given in the early days of participation at St. Rose of Lima were very helpful.

> When it was in English and they were explaining everything, I thought it was wonderful. I started learning what the Mass was all about.
>
> I enjoyed it because it enlightened me on a subject which I didn't know much about.
>
> I liked it and listened. It always bothered me not to know what they were doing at the altar.

Explanations of the Mass at sermon time on Sunday, a series of lectures, talks during Lent, talks to the children, or articles written in the parish bulletin have unquestioned value; but none has as much meaning as a commentary on the action at the very time the Mass is celebrated.

It's fine enough to explain at sermon time that this or that takes place on the altar at a particular moment but no precise *picture* is formed in the lay mind. People find it difficult to connect the isolated explanation with the particular action or moment the event takes place on the altar. Much of the Mass is still in Latin and all the motions are just so much confusion. So many things look alike. The Latin sounds so similar —one part with another. It's important to pinpoint, at the exact moment, the different things that take place. This our people found profitable. They began to relate their knowledge to what actually takes place at the altar at the particular time.

Even more important is the motivational value of spot announcements. People are aware of a need for them. The prayer of participation becomes more meaningful.

> There should be a short explanation of what the prayer is specifically about, then there will come a time when you will understand it more. You are not going to get any more out of the Mass just because you mumble so many words with the rest of the congregation.

Some commentaries need to make the hidden realities of our faith come alive. One layman expressed this point very well:

> Father X is saying Mass. If somebody got up and said, "Now Father X is making Christ present," everybody would look up. "Where is He?" Because someone is up there saying, "This is Christ up there" it has more meaning. With the explanations you stop to think and then the Mass starts to come back to you. People can't get it into their heads all by themselves that *this is Christ.*

People feel the need for more than just an intellectual understanding of the Mass. Perhaps the Mass by its very actions and words would satisfy this need, but the impact of the message shrouded in Latin words and apparently meaningless gestures is lost. The commentary becomes a necessary substitute—like a picture title flashed on a screen of a foreign movie, but it does make the picture and conversation intelligible. A good demonstration of the present lack of impact of a dramatic scene is the prayer before people's Communion, "Ecce Agnus Dei" and "Domine non sum dignus . . . " when it was said in Latin. Observe the reaction, now that it is said in English.

Regulations discourage an undue number of explanations.

This is understandable. It is, nevertheless, a reasonable interpretation of the decrees to have more commentaries in the beginning for a number of Sundays than we would normally have. It is of necessity to give the explanations, retreating from the larger number of them after a while. Too many explanations can be confusing and disturbing. Some ought to be repeated Sunday after Sunday. (It may come as a surprise, but most people don't even know the precise moment when the Consecration takes place.) The explanations have real meaning for the people. They can be phrased in a prayerful manner, and should concentrate on the principle parts of the Mass.

Commentaries

At one time I thought of composing or compiling many commentaries that we actually have made that could be used by other parishes, but this in a way would be treating others as children. It is much better if each parish composes its own. There are many excellent books written on the Mass from which priests can glean helpful thoughts. It is important for each parish to compose its own commentaries, to put them into their own words. The whole project becomes much more meaningful, to the priest, to the people. Then again, the priest becomes more alert to what the parishioners need to know about the Mass—what they're learning, what they're not. (Listen again, Fathers, to what the people tell you—what they like, what they don't like, what had much meaning for them, what had no meaning for them. This can be a pretty good, often surprisingly good, gauge.)

Eventually, some of the lay leaders should be encouraged to write out short spot commentaries. It helps them take a deeper interest in the Mass. In the beginning, the introduction of participation, especially from the aspect of explaining the Mass, normally requires a specialist in religion—a priest. We do not, however, want to rule out a qualified lay commentator. But it always takes time to form a Mass team, and while the training is going on, I see no reason why a priest cannot be used to acclimate the parish.

> . . . Instead of it being a duty, it is a privilege now.

Blessed Relief

Active participation is the emulsifier that removes part of the drudgery from the obligation of Sunday Mass. It makes worship more enjoyable. An imposed obligation rarely generates an enthusiastic spirit. It rarely gives birth to a burning ardor for a cause. A priest who might find it hard to carry out the order of his bishop to institute active participation in his parish might find it a lot easier if he foresaw constructive results in his people—the joy, the enthusiasm, the warm reception, the deep appreciation they will have for a new and active role.

Many people will find relief from the pressure of their negative feelings simply by reading the struggles of others who experienced such negative feelings toward participation at first. Even more encouraging would be actually seeing the emergence of strong positive feelings toward participation as described in this section.

On their behalf, I offer the words of our parish, as they describe their appreciation of active participation at Mass—teenagers, the aged, single, married, men, women, a cross-section of all—teachers, social workers, the butcher, the steel worker, delinquents, college graduates, a few who never even graduated from grammar school. Name the trade or the age and more than likely its words are part of these pages.

> From the time I could understand, I was told by the good nuns that if I didn't go to church, when I died the

> devils would eat me up and everything like that. It more or less grew up in me that one had to go to church. I know what it is like to feel, "Oh, I've got to go to *church* tomorrow."
>
> We weren't even thinking about Mass. We didn't get anything out of it. We were there because the Third Commandment said we had to be.
>
> I went on Sundays because I had to go. I would never have stayed away because I knew this was the law of God, but somehow it didn't seem sensible to me.
>
> You go to church sometimes and you sit there like a dummy. You go just because it is a must.
>
> Now there is no effort. Before, you used to have to tell yourself it was Sunday and you have to go to Mass. Now you more or less look forward to going because it is not a dull hour.
>
> Since I started coming to Mass here I go because I want to and get much more out of it.

Notice that people went to Church driven more by external pressures and a sense of obligation, and not from an inner conviction of the reasonableness of the worship of God. The dominant, almost exclusive, motivating force appears to be a variety of pressures: "I forced myself" or "my husband forced me," "my wife forced me," "I forced my children," and "Church pressured me through the fear of hell."

The motivating sense of obligation is expressed in a variety of ways. "We had to go," "duty," "you had to tell yourself it was Sunday and you have to go to Mass," "the Third Commandment said," "right thing to do," "must," "fulfill obligation," "sin," "pushed to go." Attending Mass in this way resulted in "a dull hour," "sit there like a dummy," "we weren't even thinking about the Mass," "little prayer," "didn't get anything out of it," "didn't seem sensible to me," "didn't understand it." It was attendance without reason—blind obedience. Such attendance surely dulls the inner spirit. The concept of Mass as an obligation creates an adverse reaction and an emotional field of repulsion.

The Law and Happiness

A biographical note on the caliber of Catholics who made such statements lends even greater weight to the values of active participation. These frank revelations of their inner feelings and thoughts were made by the "finest" of Catholics: by parents with large families who send all their children to Catholic schools—grammar, high school, many even to Catholic colleges. They are faithful to the sacraments, wouldn't think of missing Mass, cooperate in all parish undertakings and conscientiously support the parish. The street on which they live has been dubbed "Catholic Avenue." So I was enormously surprised to hear some of their statements and deeply grateful to be trusted with their inner feelings. Parallel statements have been made by a cross-section of all parishioners.

People have a different attitude toward Mass with active participation. Of course, this is not a panacea that will solve all problems of missing Mass—but a change of attitude does occur. An emotional field of attraction is generated.

The law hasn't changed, but the people's attitude toward it has.

> I've never had anything impress me so much.

People describe their reactions with expressions such as: "I really enjoy going to Church"—"no effort"—"want to go"—"get much more out of it"—"nothing like it"—"I look forward to it"—"feel better inside"—"enjoy doing it"—"I feel relaxed"—"It's alive"—"lifts you up"—"gets into you"—"never enjoyed the Mass before"—"appreciate the

Mass to a far greater extent than ever before"—"participation is great"—"privilege"—"makes one feel important"—"actually feels so big, just wonderful"—"felt quite welcome"—"feel more at home."

From Visitors

Occasionally people who were not parishioners were part of the group interviewed, and they gave their impression of the few times they had been in the parish church for the "new" Mass.

> I was very impressed, and upon leaving the Church, I felt so good—just as though I'd been to Mass for the first time.
>
> I've only attended Mass in your church once, and it gave me a warm feeling. I just hope that our church would follow the same.

A former parishioner returning to the parish after an absence of many years expressed exuberantly:

> I felt like standing up and shouting *Bravo!* It's about time you made these people pay attention to what's going on. It's about time somebody taught us what's happening. I couldn't wait until the Mass was over to rush out to tell my husband. Isn't it wonderful? It was just like someone gave us a million dollars. I wish everybody would be able to experience it. I do. I wish I could tell everybody and not say I feel sorry for them having to go to the old type of Mass. I wish everyone could have participation like we do, and I just rave about it.

We must be careful not to brand such feelings as superficial, or evaluate them lightly, or dismiss them as unlettered sentimentality. These have deep roots, to elicit such positive feelings. When adults express such things as: "I pay more attention at Mass now"—"I'm at *Mass* now, I don't know where I was before"—"My mind kept right with the Mass and right with the priest"—"We can express ourselves and understand the meaning of the Mass"—"Participation in the recited Mass gives me a feeling of belonging"—"It is a good feeling to do everything together," then we are foolish indeed not to take careful notice.

People spontaneously want to tell others about participation and express the desire to spread it to other parishes: "I wish every parish had it"—"I wish it would spread further to other parishes"—"I hope the day will come when all churches have it."

One man summarized his inner feelings: "How do *you* feel when you are upon the altar, Father? Well, we feel the same as you do—proud."

> At my parish they don't have active participation. To me, it just isn't like going to Church.

On the "Old Way"

Let us take a deeper look at the insights of our parish on non-participation.

As the interviews continued, I found many quotations were not unique and singular but began to repeat themselves frequently. It is difficult to isolate topics without anticipating new points and retouching former ones.

We can begin with an overall impression of the Mass without participation—"the emptiness"—"the nothingness."

> When I go to other churches now, it seems like I'm not even at Mass. I hardly realize what is going on. I just sit there very unhappily.
>
> Yesterday we went to St. ------ church [1] and it didn't seem like we had been to Mass.
>
> I don't think the Mass is the same if you don't participate.

[1] In almost every case, a different church is mentioned each time.

Note the *rejection* of the Mass without active participation.

> We went back to ------ church, but it was all for the birds. I was glad when it was over. I wouldn't go back there after having participation here.
>
> My son says it embarrasses him not to participate. He doesn't like it quiet. He doesn't know what is going on.

Other people tagged an un-participated Mass with "dead" —"nothing there"—"dull"—"boring"—"feel lost."

> I had something happen to me today. I went to a First Mass—a Solemn High Mass. I felt out of place. I just sat there. I got nothing out of it. I was bored.
>
> We don't go to ------ church any more because there is nothing there. I was just there. We knew why we were there, but we felt like we weren't doing anything just being there.
>
> There was no participation. I was lost.
>
> The way I feel about this is the way I feel when I go into a church where I don't understand the language they're using—like at ------ church. When I go there I feel lost because I do not understand Polish.
>
> Any time I walk into the church of my new parish, I have a sense of loss. I know very well when I walk in there, there isn't going to be a participation Mass. I know I'm going to Mass and I know I'm part of it, but somehow I don't feel right. You don't miss it until you don't have it any more. Then you realize what you've lost.
>
> It really would be dead without participation.
>
> At ----- church they don't have anything. It's quiet. It's so dead in there I feel ashamed.[2]

[2] Many others expressed similar self-consciousness and uneasiness in the quiet atmosphere of a church.

> Every time I went to Mass before, I yawned from boredom.
>
> I've been bored. I've been daydreaming when I have gone to different churches where there wasn't a participated Mass. I was just sitting there and that's it.
>
> I don't want to go back to my own church now because all I'm doing is going back to the slow hour again. I used to fall asleep. About halfway through I started yawning and continued yawning until Mass was over. Now I stay awake when I go to St. Rose.

He begs the question who says that people should be appreciating the Mass regardless of whether it is participated or not. The point of the fact is that experientially people do not seem to benefit. When they have these feelings of "being lost"—"coldness towards the Mass"—"it's dead"—"nothingness"—"emptiness"—"cut off from the altar"—"distracted"—"daydreaming"—"falling asleep"—"yawning"—who has the right to blame them?

People became very conscious of this passivity at un-participated Mass. They described it in a variety of ways:

> In the summer we go to . . . . We go to church there and the priest is real nice. When we attend Mass there, I honestly feel like I'm watching television because they do not have participation. I'm just watching and watching and watching. Actually you feel as if you didn't go to church at all. When you don't have participation, you just sit there—nothing. With participation, I guess most people enjoy it more. You want to come back.

The Central Mystery

Strange that a parish should look upon the central mystery of their Faith as something so spiritless, so empty, so boring, so full of distraction. And yet it is a fact. Hence, one great value of participation is that it can rectify the people's outlook toward the Mass, and thus towards their Faith in Christ and in the Church.

At an un-participated Mass, people experienced coldness, and felt like strangers.

> I've been to a church that had participation, but only certain responses were expected of the congregation. But even that was a little better than the "professional Mass" where the choir and the priest participate, but that's all. You feel like an outsider. I couldn't take part in it. I didn't feel like I was there and that I was interested in it.

> I went to a beautiful church once and they had a choir in the balcony. Everybody was looking around to see where the music was coming from. For every part of the Mass they had a different soloist. It was a huge church, but you felt left out. We were all the way in the back and you just couldn't feel a part of anything.

> Without participation you become a critic of everything they do. If they have a choir, in your estimation they don't know how to sing. When they do sing, they don't sing the way they are supposed to be singing and so forth.

By way of observation, a person doesn't usually become a critic if he takes part in the performance. He should tend, all things being equal, to gloss over his own failings—but when someone else is performing, he has a tendency to become a critic, observe and pass judgment.

Now we can't blame anybody for rejecting the Mass if this is the way they experience it, if the overall effect is that they haven't even gone to church—felt empty about it—thought it was dead—felt confused—lost—didn't know where they were —cut off from the altar—cut off from everybody else—felt distracted—found it hard to concentrate—daydreamed—yawned—slept—bored. People felt like strangers in the very place where they should have felt at home.

> Everybody walks in alone and walks out alone. You don't feel any closeness. You're alone in a crowd.

Isolation and the Community

Isolation is a phenomenon of present-day city life. People live too close to one another, and at the same time do not know their neighbors, next door, in the apartment above, in the apartment alongside. Sometimes a man withdraws from society, a withdrawal from life that frequently leads to a mental institution. Thus, the implicit tragedy of worship that tends to spawn aloneness and isolation. A formal worship that engenders such isolation amidst a crowd is certainly contrary to the true worship of the Mystical Body of Christ: this liturgy fails ritually in its purpose of drawing man to man and man to God.

This feeling of aloneness was threaded all through the comments describing non-participated Mass. The awareness of these feelings contrasted sharply with the positive feelings of togetherness expressed after active participation.

> I went to St. ------ church before I went to St. Rose, and it seemed like everyone was by himself, in his own secluded corner. They were not doing anything together.

> When you go to a church that doesn't have the recited Mass, you're alone, you're really by yourself. I sort of get the feeling there is me and God, and that I'm praying alone and so is everybody else.

> In a quiet Mass it seems like just one person, the priest, is offering the Mass, whereas in the recited Mass there is a greater unity. The prayers of the people are all flow-

> ing together instead of all going off in separate directions.
>
> In other places, the Mass belongs to the priest. That is his job. He says the Mass and that's it. We listen. But here it belongs to everybody. People gather together to worship together. It's the greatest feeling.

Shall we quietly accept the fact that people must suffer such isolation-in-a-crowd—in the *Church*, where everyone is supposed to experience the unity and familiarity of a family, where we are to experience the Mystical Body at home in our Father's house? Our parish expressed the same thought in so many different ways it cannot be denied. "By yourself." "Alone in a crowd." "Work as a single unit." "Secluded corner." "Own little mood." "All wrapped up." "So detached." We walked in alone, walked out alone, and so we lived alone, worked alone, and for all practical purposes we *were* alone.

How gratifying it was to hear people say, "My neighbor is no longer a stranger." As we listened to the people, we found that those who experienced active participation at Mass grew in awareness that the Mass is community worship—the public worship of the Mystical Body of Christ. As one person put it:

> You can't appreciate the idea of community when you read a book about it—when you read about the unified feeling of the people and the priest as their representative. You couldn't get that feeling, that sense of being in the Mystical Body.

Through active participation, many people experienced a closeness to the priest-president and their fellow parishioners. So many expressed how the bonds of union with one another and with the celebrant became an existential reality, a conscious experience.

> When you're participating altogether it seems like all the people belong together, that you are all part of a

family. We're all together, singing together, offering the Mass together with the priest. He's not the whole show. We're all in it together.

When I go to another church where it is not a recited Mass, I feel like we are a thousand parts, all separate. When you walk in, you're just a little piece. Somehow when you walk into St. Rose's you walk into this unity.

When you have participation it is all the people honoring God the same way. It makes you feel more a part of the whole Church in terms of people. There is more of a connection between the priest, myself and the people 'round me. You realize the Church is not just a building but rather is composed of people.

The Catholic Church consisted of nuns and priests. Now since the recited Mass, we all say the "Amens" together, all the responses. People are one with the Church. Before if the Church was crowded, there would be 500 individuals there.

I couldn't feel any unity in the Church. I was told that the priest is offering Mass for me, but I couldn't see any connection how he was doing it for me. Now every time the priest turns around and says "Dominus vobiscum" and 500 people shout out "Et cum spiritu tuo," I can *see* it. He's talking directly to you. Before he was just talking to those few altar boys around him and the people were just shoved aside. I feel like the priest is saying "Come closer." I feel a real closeness. I experience the unity.

I like participating with the congregation as well as actually feeling that at the same time I am participating with the priest. I don't feel like I'm up there at the altar performing, but I feel that he is part of me and I am part of him. All of us in a sense are in the same position as the priest is at the altar. Participation in the recited Mass is the best thing that ever happened.

> You're enjoying the Mass more because you're participating with the priest saying the Mass.

As individualistic worship could produce nothing more than an individualistic activity, so community worship will lead us to community activity, *a natural outgrowth* of our community worship. Our parish came alive because we worshiped as a family. We did nothing more than respect, and accept for what it is, the official Christian life of prayer.

[6]

Time and Time Again

It seems that you no sooner walk into the church, and you're on your way out. The time is the same, but the interest in the Mass makes the time go by a lot faster. It doesn't drag out.

OUR people expressed many such positive feelings after exposure to active participation, in bold relief to the negative attitudes which complained "alone," "dead," "lost," "missing," "spectator," "watching," "dummy," "boring," and so forth and so on of the 'dead' Mass. Of the many reactions, I was struck by the number who brought in the element of time, in describing the differences between the participated Mass and the unparticipated. Let it be said now:

For the Mass without participation, "went slow," "longer than an hour, it seemed," "kept wondering if it was ever going to be over," "went on forever and ever," "seems so long," "tends to drag," "get tired," "just waiting to get it over with," and a host of equivalents gave voice to deeply rooted negative feelings which made me wonder why most of them ever bothered to go to Mass at all. The *time* element (and we have more to say about that for the consolation of all those priests who have heard these complaints so many times themselves) was one of the easiest points of comparison.

For instance, these are typical of the remarks on participation which usually accompanied the above:

> Naturally, if you don't understand something, it's very boring to you, and it goes on forever. When you ac-

> tively participate, you understand more. The time goes faster and it is more enjoyable.
>
> I used to wonder when and if the Mass was ever going to be over. Before the recited Mass when I did go to church, it was a matter of just waiting until it was time to get out.
>
> With participation it doesn't seem like it did before, when the half hour or forty-five minutes used to just drag.
>
> It seems like Mass is only twenty minutes or so, and here it is an hour sometimes.

Priests have been made extremely self-conscious in regard to how much time Mass takes. Many are frankly afraid to say Mass slowly, lest the inevitable flood of complaints begin. How many a newly ordained priest has learned this lesson within the first few days of his ministry! How many assistants have been rushed by the pastor, who is sincerely trying to spare his parishioners whatever it is that causes the adverse reactions he knows will be coming? ("We can't keep these poor people in there *forever*.")

Yet, adverse reaction is *not* based on the amount of time it actually takes to offer Mass, but from the type of Mass itself. Said as rapidly as possible, an unparticipated Mass draws the same comments—"drag," "boredom," "relief to get out of there." Conversely, a priest dare not gallop through a Mass if the parish is working with him. He is literally forced to take his time, to say everything more devoutly—and God's people love it.

A Little Understanding

In making that statement, we are of course presupposing the careful mechanical preparation that went into our parish liturgical revival. The best of intentions and most articulate of arguments will be dissipated by a badly handled set of mechanics—poorly delivered readings, commentaries and sermons; an awkward organist; hymns geared more for the feminine taste than the masculine. These are accidentals, it may be argued, but in the same sense, it is precisely the "accidentals" of the liturgy with which this entire movement is concerned.

Even when the accidentals, the mechanics, of the unparticipated liturgy are well handled—as they were in our parish, by the way—why were the feelings of our people so negative? There seems to be no question now that they enjoyed and appreciated the participated liturgy precisely *because they could understand it*. Even those who resisted active participation the most vigorously echoed this thought: "I understand the Mass more now." The next step in their development was to *enjoy* it; we hope now, after several years, that most of them have come to freely and consciously *love* it. St. Thomas' principle is still shrewdly valid: *nihil volitum nisi cognitum*—nothing is willed until it is known.

When the personal knowledge of it is inadequate, inaccurate and confused, it is not surprising that the Mass also becomes unattractive. Like a picture on a slide projector, out of focus, not only is its beauty impossible to appreciate, it is disturbing to the onlooker. Either we adjust the projector, or we move on to something else. Laymen, however, were not free to correct their blurred picture of the Mass, and many of them reacted adversely to it. Some others moved away from it, and for many of those who stayed on, what kept them there was a sense of obligation (which is admirable and even a little touching), or the threat of hell-fire (which is pathetic).

The more it is possible for a person to experience the Mass as it unfolds, the more its different parts are linked together, the more he sees it as "good, true and beautiful," and the more he comes to love it. The stress on *experience* in that statement is quite deliberate. One can read several superb explanations of the Mass, attend a lecture series by a leading authority and still, when one comes to Mass, be unable to integrate this cerebral material into a living experience. When the Mass presents a clear picture, it can be seen as the truth which it is, and it is no longer disturbing. (In the next few pages, we will see that an alarming number of people came to Mass and deliberately, if in the best of conscience, *ignored* the confusing jumble in front of them for the security and comforts of a Rosary.) A clear picture initiates a positive reaction—positive *emotional* reaction is the better term, and not to be dismissed as superficial because it springs from a better understanding of the Faith.

Participation brings people into a new world, or so they told me. They find a wonderful exuberance, and vitality, and enthusiasm in this new world. So their descriptions came in terms of what they now "knew," or saw, felt and heard. "Understanding is the main thing, that's what it is." "Gives the Mass a deeper meaning." "I understand the Mass so much better." "Get more out of it." "Learn more about the Mass just through doing it." "Changing everybody's idea of what the Mass actually is." By the theologian's standards, it is not unfair to remark how very little these people know about the Mass even now. For our purposes, I think it is most sufficient to wonder: What must have been their knowledge *before* . . . ?

Here are several quotes which will bring these thoughts into clearer focus.

> I went to Mass because I had to go and that was it, but I didn't understand anything at all about it until they started this recited Mass with the explanations. I didn't know what was taking place at the altar before at all. I had no idea what the priest was doing.

> This is a painless learn-as-you-go-along thing. It isn't as demanding as spending two evenings a week on an instruction-type of thing. You learn as you go. It's go-

> ing to Mass and *getting an education* . . . as well as becoming more a part of what you are trying to do in church.
>
> It is a wonderful idea because this way you know just exactly how to stay with the priest. It gives you more of an idea of what the Mass is all about and I just love it, really and truly.

A number of people expressed the idea that what they had learned from participation helped them to attend non-participated Mass more prayerfully and with greater understanding.

> You can go to almost any church now and follow the priest. You will understand the Mass because of your own experience.

Some like to imagine that Catholic school training suffices to give a person a sufficient knowledge of the Mass—but this isn't so. People with a thorough Catholic training expressed the following:

> The good part of it is that now you understand the Mass. We went to Catholic schools and didn't understand the Mass. If the priest at the altar crossed himself, so did we, just like little monkeys. We didn't understand why. Now when we cross ourselves, we know *why* we do it.

Priests in neighborhoods where a good number send their children to public schools, for whatever reason, will find the participation taking on added importance in the light of our failures in catechetical instruction:

> I went to a public school and didn't know one end of the Mass from the other.
>
> I'm sure I missed some of the things that the children get in the Catholic schools. I think this is rather a strong point because not everyone can attend a Catholic school.

> No matter if all the Catholics wanted to send their children to Catholic schools, there is not enough room to do this. Therefore, this kind of Mass they have at St. Rose's will help those of us who did not get this early training. I am more appreciative and aware of getting more out of the Mass at St. Rose. I feel more comfortable attending Mass here than I do elsewhere, in the sense that I have an opportunity to feel where I am going, what's coming, what's happening.

A convert's insight on the personal values of active participation is significant:

> I have the convert's point of view. I like it because I can understand the Mass. I know what's going on now.

We might wonder too what there is in a participated liturgy that helps bring people back into the Church, that draws back the fallen-away. . . .

> It gave the Mass a deep meaning. Now I understand my religion much more clearly. This never would have been possible without the recited Mass.

> I was away from the Church for many years. Eight years ago you people started telling me what the Mass was all about. That's when I really got honestly excited. For the first time in my life, I wanted to learn what the Mass really is.

People come to love participation because it adds to their understanding of the Mass, a weighty reason in itself for their wanting more of it, and a reinforcement of the principle given by the Council document when it speaks of the liturgy as a "teacher." We want to make the worship of Christians total and, of course, rational. If people are aware of what is going on, we are assured that the rational machinery of man is in operation. It is interesting to note (once more) that when the topic of active participation was brought up, the first evaluation was usually in terms of *understanding* the Mass. It became something of a refrain, in fact.

I sense here the fragmentary expression of a nameless depth of meaning. I am always aware of it as I hear our people express themselves in the living context of the liturgy. I have heard priests who fear that participation can never be more than another external operation. But our parish was not referring to mere externals when it said, over and over again,

> This has brought me understanding of the Mass. And this is why I appreciate it, and enjoy it.

Distractions, Ho

> "No time to catnap." "Daydream." "Gawk around." "Get carried away." "You're really in there, you're concentrating."

The effect of active participation on distractions came up almost as frequently as the question of better understanding the Mass—even more frequently in some respects. People said they understood the Mass more and were able to follow it more *closely, more prayerfully,* with fewer *distractions.* Frankly, this was a stunning revelation when it finally dawned on me. I had never questioned what I thought would be the added distractions—that would be and must be tolerated for other values gained—which participation would impose on our people.

It came as a surprise, then, to be told that people preferred participation because they were less distracted. "Keeps your mind on the altar, right on the Mass." "Keeps you on your toes." "Alert." "You know that you are really paying attention." "Nothing else is on your mind." "Would doze off—but not now!" "No trouble staying awake." The contrast drawn between participated and non-participated Mass was sharp and clear: "Used to float away into space thinking of everything else"—"my mind wanders"—"I'm not really paying attention to the Mass"—"I used to watch everybody come in."

The priest wrestles with the problem of distractions in his personal life, and in the lives of people he guides. He preaches on distractions, counsels in the confessional and in the parlor on the importance of fighting distractions in prayer. It is eminently logical, therefore, that he ought to be laboring zealously and fearlessly to banish the environment of the "dead" Mass which spawns distractions so easily and uniformly in the lives of his parishioners. If he does not, I think the reason is *not* a shortage of good will and dedication, so much as it is a wanting of personal experience and reflection.

It isn't an easy job to accept this fact of distractions against the background of a seminary training. It is an easy step to assume that lay people have the same facility for mental prayer in a quiet atmosphere.

Priests have a fight with distractions when it has come time to take their Mass and share it with a congregation. But the priest's problem is not the problem of the congregation: Silence seems to foster daydreaming, they told me. People in a large group are easily distracted by quiet. They find it difficult, if not impossible, to meditate. Their unanimous experience, from our interviews, was this: active participation does not distract me from prayer, but helps me to concentrate.

Priests must still urge and exhort their people to meditate. There are certain parts of the Mass, indeed, when this is precisely what they (and the priest with them) should be doing. What, after all, is the purpose of the Gradual and Tract, coming after the Epistle reading, if not a *meditative* reflection on what they have just heard? Should not all of us meditate just before we receive the Body of the Lord? When it is time to pray together, good. When it is time to pray privately, good . . . because the Lord expects both kinds of prayer from us.

Against the background and training of their lives as laymen, most people are not able to meditate, at first. It is surprising, and intriguing, to watch them learn to meditate, from their experience of formally and *meaningfully* praying (for the first time, one suspects). Listen to some of their comments:

> I like participation because I really am getting the meaning of the words. Otherwise I would be gawking around saying a few Hail Mary's. I would even forget the Mass was going on.
>
> I would say the Rosary, and I would look at a cute hat and notice who had a new dress and wonder when it was going to be over. And then I was out. Now it's different. It's *altogether* different.

And this light-hearted and wonderfully honest description of her past ways:

> Well, I mean for me the Mass was a hectic blur. I would get in Church, you know, and I'd look at the candles. I didn't even know what kind of Mass it was. I'd sit on the bench, and I'd look at the candles. Then I'd think, Gee, that's a cute little altar boy. Now what's Father doing? I'd say a prayer and my knees would hurt. I'd just get comfortable on the bench and then, Oh, for heaven's sake, do I have to stand up *again?* I've got to get out of this place.
>
> Now what is he talking about? Good Lord, I don't know what he's saying. When is the next holyday? Are they going up for Communion?
>
> I mean, this was what was going through my mind all the time. I'd get up and get down again. I'd look at the confessional. I'd follow every painting. I'd get comfortable on the bench. My husband used to poke me in the ribs—Will you PLEASE sit *still!* Well, you know, then I'd get mad. . . . Honestly, I used to get out of church a nervous wreck, from all that movement and fighting and all, in church!

It is revealing here to examine a little deeper how a quiet atmosphere gave birth to distractions. I could not help but compare the picture these people painted of quiet with the much different one I had.

> When it was quiet in the Church I would daydream, but with everybody participating, I'm trying to participate with the rest. You don't intentionally get carried away from the Mass, you just do. . . . Something comes to your mind and if you're in a quiet part of the Mass, you'll be daydreaming. It's hard to pray that way for an hour, all by yourself.

> For forty-five minutes to just sit, concentrate and follow the Mass is just too hard for anybody. There are always distractions. I forget what's going on and start to think of something else and not follow it. . . . With participation, you have less chance to get distracted.

> When it's very quiet on Sunday, unless I'm very careful, I think to myself, Oh, what am I going to do when I get home—or I'm listening to someone banging their rosary beads, or the quietness of it all.

Some were conscious that they had been making an effort for years to participate with a Missal. This was participating, of course, but by oneself:

> Before active participation I got carried away. Even reading, I got distracted easily. This way when I am participating in the Mass it seems so much easier to follow than when I pray by myself. I wish every parish had it.

Not everyone felt that participation completely eliminated the tendency to wander. Many appreciated the ways in which the role assigned to the congregation would snap them back to attention. One man speaks of his need of an "undistractor." (In a very special sense, every "Dominus vobiscum" supplies this. I doubt not that this may have been the original purpose of this greeting, that it drew the congregation back into the action.)

> It's the same old story—you watch people come in, you look at women's hats. If you have participation, it brings you back to what you're supposed to be paying attention to. It's an "un-distractor." It brings you back to the Mass. But if you have a non-participation Mass, you can't just keep from being distracted, so you'll go from one thing to another.
>
> When you are actually participating you hear the words as well as see them. How can you be remote under those circumstances? It's a physical impossibility.
>
> Before, many times, years ago, I found myself just sitting idly thinking about other things and I would get a million miles away from the Mass. But participation keeps demanding my attention. It helps me to think of what I actually should be thinking about.

The ushers are in an excellent position to observe the congregation's attentiveness, before and after participation:

> I have been attending Mass for over forty years, twenty-nine of them as an usher. This puts me in a good position to observe the people at Mass. There were some people, I might say a few, who would be reading their missals or saying the Rosary. There were far more looking at the ceiling or watching out the window at what the neighbors were doing and what they were wearing. It was every person for himself, in an attitude of "We can't wait until it gets over." Not any more—everyone is praying and singing together, cooperating 100% with the priest, saying the Mass and no one leaves until the last song has been sung. It's a beautiful togetherness.
>
> I notice that there isn't as much bobbing and weaving around as people are coming into the church. Before when somebody came to church late with high heels

that "click, click, click," the first thing you know heads would be snapping around to see who was coming. I don't see this very much any more. People are more interested in what they are doing.

Before, the people went to church for forty-five minutes because they had to be there. Now I notice that if you look at their faces, they're more interested and don't have the dull expression they used to have. They'd come to church half asleep and go out still half asleep. People are more awake in church now than they were before. They have an expression on their face that they know what's going on and they look at the altar more. Before they had their eyes in their books and some were actually dozing off. With active participation in the Mass the children are more occupied and less restless, than at another church where they just have to sit there.

Achievement

You've climbed a step. You've had a lift.

To conclude this discussion, we should take into consideration the basic human drive towards a reasonable independent achievement: the sense of satisfaction which always accompanies the job well done. This is good, and reasonable, and needs no defense in any other sphere. It was such a part of our parish's self-evaluation of our reformed liturgy that we cannot omit it here.

Active participation does bring about a notable measure of this sense of accomplishment in the person's attitude towards the Mass. People felt that they had contributed something, that they had *accomplished* something. When an adult has undergone a meaningless experience, he does not have such a reaction. Our people grasped something solid, although to say this is not really enough. At any rate, they were "part of the Mass," and had "really gone through something," or "got so much more out of it," and "were really praying."

Part of this sense of achievement was the awareness that they were responsible for the action of the Mass. Ontologically, of course, we realize that the intimate union between Christ the High Priest and the faithful is complete—but does the layman in the world of experience really *feel* such closeness? Does he sense that he is a part of the Mass without active participation, or does this become a relatively meaningless matter of ontology, too? No question that active participation in our parish brought the person "in," and made him a part "of" the Mass:

> My home parish doesn't have active participation. To me, it just doesn't seem like going to church there. I feel more like I have gone to church when I come here. We really worship. You've done more when you come here.

> Sometimes I feel that the priest is doing his part and I am doing mine. Our parts together—that's fine. To me, I go to church now and if there is no recited Mass or sung Mass, the Mass is nothing. I have often wondered—all these years—did I ever fulfill my obligation? Just because I went there? Why did I go? I didn't give anything. I didn't receive anything. How could I fulfill my obligation? By taking up space? Is it a rule of the Church to go to church to occupy space!
>
> I don't see it that way. Now I know I participate. I feel better. I go to church now and if I don't have active participation I get bored—even if I went through all the motions and received Holy Communion, I wouldn't be able to say I really went to church. I was there. I went to Holy Communion but was I in *church*?

> Another church was closer to my home, but I didn't care for it. You just went and came back. You didn't give yourself, or something. I don't know. You just . . . attended.

> I feel that when I go to Mass I am giving something of myself—that I've been part of the Mass, not sitting there like a dummy while somebody else is doing my work. I feel I'm being heard, that I'm not being left out.

One wonders what they felt before, whether perhaps they were like the player sitting on the bench. He never got into the game. "I'm part of the team, but I never get to play." A person needs to get into the game.

Priests, I suppose, are not as appreciative of this thought as they should be. It has a direct bearing on the Mass. We are all in the game, and we are always playing. The star player always has a hard time understanding the feelings of the man on the bench, unless he has sat there for a long time himself. But that is not the fate of the usual priest: he is priest-president, and the "game" cannot be a real *game,* a contest, unless he is in it.

The negative feelings our people expressed, as being spectators, were in marked contrast to their positive pleasure at suddenly becoming *part* of something. The really great accomplishments of the Mass lie in the realms of divine grace. And yet we are setting up a monstrous dichotomy when man at worship is treated as though he worshiped only with a soul and not with his entire being. It is good when a man experiences ritually the accomplishment, and satisfaction, and honest joy, which are all part of the Christian mystery of the Mass.

A sensitivity to a man's need to have a sense of accomplishment is part of all our responsibility here. It makes the practical matters of liturgical reform much easier to plot out. Its reward is its own sense of satisfaction that we can involve the whole man, the total man, the psychosomatic unity, in the Christian experience of worshiping God. After all, that's how God made us all: and grace still has a habit of building on human nature. That fact, indeed, is one of the greatest mysteries of the redemption wrought in Christ Jesus.

[7]

Who Likes Singing?

THERE are few people still left in actively promoting the liturgical renewal who will not stress the terrific—enormous—importance in a satisfying liturgy of song *by* the community. There are fewer still who do not by now recognize the vast practical difficulties involved in getting a community to sing with any enthusiasm. But there are too many who beg off in the face of these difficulties, with sighs of resignation and a show of disappointment that "people just won't sing in Church."

We flatly disagree. People will sing—provided certain essential mechanical details are attended to. Among these must be included such matters as a separate approach to as many men in the parish as can be reached, a capable organist (and a decent instrument on which to play—sooner or later we must face up to this fact), and sound, virile, aesthetically pleasing music to sing. A leader of song, provided for in the Liturgy Constitution, is an excellent aid to the congregation as it begins to develop; this is another area in which there is much experimenting to be done. The "cantor" is another link between priest and people, and perhaps the most valuable one conceivable, especially in the next few years as we begin the process of inserting our own language into the Eucharistic celebration. The entire community—priest and people—singing the Sanctus, or the Agnus Dei, or the Gloria, or the Creed, now makes the song of the community strikingly manifest as a liturgical action. This degree of complexity requires a particular kind of leadership. A cantor at a separate microphone is a fitting and easy way around the difficulty.

With these details attended to, the majority of people desire, approve of, and enjoy singing at Mass on Sundays. After a time, perhaps a year or two, it is not unusual to find the congregations at even the early morning, weekday Masses breaking into song. Music is by nature festive, and it is enjoyable once people can relax with it. Here is a list of statements of approval which we can multiply into the hundreds:

> I could sing all the time. I express myself better in singing. I love to sing.
>
> I like to sing. If I'm not allowed to sing, I feel like I have been cheated.
>
> . . . lost without it.
>
> I don't respond myself until the singing part comes along. Now this, as they say in the modern age, *I dig.* Ninety out of a hundred people like to sing. You know what I like best? Christmas, because you sing more songs.
>
> In the Protestant churches they participate so much. They really sing. I always felt this was what was lacking in the Catholic churches.

Surprising, but those statements were made by men. Even those who objected in general to the whole idea of participation wanted to retain the singing of carols during the Christmas season and hymns appropriate to Easter; in fact, I found scarcely one person who objected to carols, or even a recessional hymn.

Singing—contrary to some peculiar polls taken in other places—was so readily accepted that we found little or no opposition to it. Perhaps in those parishes which find opposition to singing the answer is to examine just what *kind* of a total approach to participation is being used. I stress the kind of approach. Singing was an important part of a program of worship which our parish adopted on its own approval. I would have been quite surprised to find that the inspiring noises we made together every *Sunday* were not at the same time something we all seemed to enjoy so much. The enthusiastic responses to questions on singing were full of deep, personal insights. Here are some of the others:

> The more singing at Mass, the better.
>
> Gives vent to your feelings by singing, otherwise it is a monologue. There is so much more meaning to song itself.
>
> When you know a song by heart, you go out singing it. You feel like it isn't quiet prayer: It's a *loud* prayer. A lot of times you want to bring out your prayers in voice.
>
> . . . feel happier and better when I sing.
>
> You express yourself better with singing. Maybe you can't say it in words, through speaking. But singing, you can say so much more. Singing is a must.
>
> . . . you are participating more.

People were much more aware of the unity, the oneness, that results from singing.

> . . . one group, one song, one purpose.
>
> Gives you a feeling of belonging.
>
> Everyone joining in the singing really makes you feel that you are a part of the service.

Others spoke of singing as making them less distracted:

> You're less prone to distractions if you can burst out into song periodically. It helps break down people's reserve when they sing. Singing brings you back into the Church and you feel better. You feel more at Mass.
>
> I'd rather have the congregation sing instead of the choir. I noticed at High Mass it seems you follow along

> with the choir and you get distracted because you're listening to them sing. It would be better if the whole congregation sang during the Mass.

There was an interesting variation expressed, as to how preferable singing, as a prayer form, was to anything else. Many people preferred congregational singing to public prayer, and some contrasted it with past experiences as choir members. But the point came clearly across: they were personally *conscious* of the fact that community singing was real prayer, and they liked it.

> I like praying with the congregation, but not as much as singing.

> Now I enjoy the singing more than I did when I used to go to Church and sing as a choir member.

Most people preferred singing as a congregation to listening to a choir.

> I don't think having a choir is fair. Everyone should be allowed to sing.

> If the choir is singing, I'm left out. You sit there and mentally sing, which really doesn't amount to anything.

> I really want to sing. I don't want to listen. I don't want a choir.

Some people did enjoy a good choir, of course, and were disappointed that we no longer had an excellent choir at St. Rose. At one time we did have a show-piece choir—men and boys, and good, four-part singing. They attained some degree of excellence, and were well thought of. But slowly the men began to drop out, practices became burdensome, no recruits stepped in to take the place of those who had left. Under such pressures, the choir faded out of existence.

We have a sort of choir now, an offshoot of the group which helped introduce the congregational singing. These men chant the Propers when we have Latin High Masses. We have plans to use them for more complicated psalms and other things, relating to the Propers as they become prayers in English. For recited Masses, there is surely no reason against the use of a choir to augment or dress up hymn singing; contrasted here with the use of a large group of men in the body of the church whose function is to bolster (lead, really) hymn singing in its first stages.

Many authorities stress the importance of a choir. We do not say have no choirs. But at the first stages of participation, stressing the development of the choir is putting the cart before the horse. Sometimes a choir becomes "my choir," a pet project of pastor or organist, who is innocently caught—a victim of personal drive for a sense of accomplishment or achievement, blinding him from seeing a choir as an integral part of the community singing and rather setting up a conflict: choir vs. community song. In this way, congregational singing poses a threat to many a choir. It is wise to discuss and explore at length the role of a choir in the church and how it can dovetail with community song. As congregational singing develops, some people, as a natural consequence, will want to give of themselves more fully to the praise of God through song. In the most natural way possible, a choir can mushroom, effortlessly, out of the new needs of the community's song. When it becomes absolutely necessary to add the richness, excitement and beauty of a choir to the community's song, then the choir has become the product *of the community,* and the community welcomes them.

This is a far different matter from having a choir which is designed to "cover up" the supposed crudeness of a congregation which is just learning to sing.

More High Masses?

Then too there is the question of what to do with a choir

at anything other than a Latin High Mass. The people to consult here are the professional musicians, but we can testify to the wonderful quality of harmony which can be added, through simple one and two part descants, to otherwise ordinary hymns. The addition of descants gives a familiar hymn, like *Holy God,* a new life. Descants add *excitement* to hymns, a desirable quality which we seem to ignore when talking about congregational singing. A good, solid hymn is a prayer —and the more exciting a prayer it is, the better. We might add that there is no reason why the choir cannot be seated in the body of the congregation. What can be accomplished in placing the choir downstairs is the reunification of the community under the leadership of the priest and cantor. This arrangement also adds much to the singing.

Within this context, a negligible number of our parishioners, as few as 5 out of the 383 interviewed, had any objections to singing. This, I think, is surprisingly small.

> I don't care for singing. When I go to Church, it's to *pray*—not sing. I'm not a singer, and I don't ever intend to be one!

> I enjoy perfection. I don't like to hear anybody sing who can't sing.

Others brought up difficulties related to the work involved in singing:

> . . . too timid to try to sing out.

> If you can't pronounce the words, you can't sing with the others. You feel left out.

These are problems,[1] and the honesty with which these problems were revealed is itself encouraging. But for the others, the overwhelming majority, music was something which brought them together. It spanned oceans, crossed na-

[1] See pages 35-46 for a fuller expression of people's difficulties regarding singing, participation, etc.

tional boundaries, erased color lines. Singing was a link with our separated brothers, and it helped the adjustment process of new Catholics:

> I learned "Holy God" at the Moody Bible Institute when I was six years old. Doesn't that bring a unity to everything?

That's a good question, and one which will have to be answered by others. But in that remark, and in others, music was described in terms of having a natural and easy carry-over into the daily lives of our parish. Singing brought the Church into their homes:

> Over and above the other things, my husband, daughter and I love to sing anyway. If we are doing the dishes or cleaning walls or something, we sing popular songs. But it isn't uncommon for us now to come up with the Gloria, or the Kyrie, Sanctus or "Holy God" or any of the things we sing in Church. It just comes out spontaneously. But we never did this before.

> A lot of things you forget. The singing seems to bring it all back to your mind. All day long the songs keep coming back to you.

> My oldest daughter is only two and a half. We were putting her to bed the other night and I told her to kneel down and say her prayers. "I don't want to say my prayers," she said. So I said, "Well, what *do* you want to do?" She was perfectly dead-pan: "I don't want to say my prayers. I want to *sing* like we do in church." So I said to go right ahead. Very solemnly, she sang the last verse of "Here We Go 'Round the Mulberry Bush," the one about "This is the way we go to church / so early Sunday morning."

Such specific values which people express on the subject of liturgical song run parallel to the values they express on participation itself. Quite often, participation and song are but one thing: people enjoy participation because they enjoy singing, and the reverse. People are less distracted because they can participate, and priests especially must never forget this. It would be difficult to measure the proportions of preference for praying together, as against singing together, but the percentages would be decidedly in favor of singing.

The Church wants participation at every Mass, a holy activity which brings joy and satisfaction to every man, woman and child. Song must certainly be a prominent part of their worship.

[8]

A New Breed of Layman

When people see a layman in the position of commentator, it's like a link between the priest and the people.

THE United States has been spared to an overwhelming degree the terrible scourge of anti-clericalism which has so dogged the Catholicism of European countries. Yet many scholars have noted the beginnings of a subtle form of anti-clericalism in this country. Msgr. John Tracy Ellis warned of some of the symptoms in a recent address, suggesting that anti-clerical sentiments hitherto unknown to American Catholicism have begun to spread among the ranks of the most vigorous laity in the universal Church.[1]

Anti-clericalism presupposes the existence of "clericalism," and so I suppose to be fair the clergy should do their own share of self-examination. The implications of anti-clericalism on the parish liturgical reform are frightening, however. When there is an unhealthy tension between the priest and the people of a parish, it would be foolish to try to foster mutual cooperation. And yet this is precisely what participated liturgy *must* have in order to exist, and develop. Apart from formal anti-clericalism, an alarming "distance" or separation most often exists between clergy and laity. This sense of separation has created an image of the Church expressed by one man in these words:

> In this Church, it was strictly the priest alone.

Or, *this* one . . .

[1] *The New World* (Chicago, Illinois), June, 1962.

> I think it has been a fault of the Catholic Church that the laity is forgotten except for fund-raising purposes!

Those indictments imply the kind of image which aggravates the virus of anti-clericalism. It quite effectively tears apart the holy Body of Christ. It makes impossible the clergy-laity "team" which is essential for handling the mechanics of participation, although we have no intention of making mechanics the sole *ratio* of parish liturgy as embracing priest and specially trained laymen. But the commentators themselves were unanimous in speaking of the lay commentator as bridging the gulf between priest and people, as establishing a bond which united everyone.

> There is a great breach between the clergy and the people. Commentating by laymen is breaking down this vast gulf. It's a bridge that is bringing priest and people closer together . . . at least a little bit.

> A lot of criticism disappeared after you made laymen commentators. This is a big selling point.

> You are no longer an individual. You become a part. You are right along with the priest where you never were before.

> I'm honored that I can do a thing like this. I don't like to say that it puts me on the level with the priest, but it does bring me closer. Commentating brings about a perfect relationship for the lay people in the Church. It is a link between the layman and the Mass.

In other words, their very presence within the confines of the sanctuary broke down the barriers. "Barriers" is the exact word, although the reality involved may be only a psychological one. Many times I have heard priests complain that they "couldn't get participation started," and on further questioning I learned that they, the priests, were doing the commentating; and it didn't work.

Priests, I confess, too often overlook the values of laymen within the very organizational structure of the Church. But when this happens in the parochial liturgy, it is particularly unfortunate. When the commentator is a layman, the organizational Church takes on a new image. There is cooperation, there is sharing, there is friendship—and there should be all these things, and there is no reason on earth or in heaven why there should not be.

In the times to come when our liturgy will gradually become a reality *of* our own language, the assumption is often that the need for commentators will be eliminated. We would agree, on the surface, to the statement. We do not agree that the need for active laymen *in* the liturgy, fulfilling a kind of *ministerial* function—in the words of the liturgy Constitution—will ever again become unnecessary. As one man put it,

> There is a definite advantage to spreading the job around.

Indeed there is. One of the common advantages mentioned regarded the "preachy" tone which priests often use—but which the lay commentator would not dare use. People sense many things about the presence of laymen as commentators, and one of the most notable is the distinction between the priest preaching, and the commentator leading. "Preaching" here has a pejorative undertone which has nothing to do with the sermon or homily because the sermon is still a high point in "their" liturgy. But our parish expressed their natural resentment at "constantly being told what to do." This holds true for us all; we resent preaching, but not so much do we resent being led. Many, many times we are grateful for good leadership, something which comes rather naturally to people who have tasted the good air of democracy. The priest at Mass is *the* leader of the assembly of God's people. One of the prime duties of the commentator is to assist the priest in his priestly work, and in this sense, he helps the priest lead.

The commentator is a layman. Yet he is by his presence assisting the priest because the priest is officially the "president" of this assembly and is "superior" to everyone else. Therefore the commentator is not exactly on a par with the congregation, yet he is subordinate to the celebrant. He is a mediator. He has a special dignity as a layman. He is a special layman. We can return to that point again, but this cooperation between the priest, the "ministers," and the community has a special effect on bringing the community closer to the holy action of the Mass:

> In the service, a guy would rather hang around with a bunch of privates than he would with his sergeant. This is a similar situation. When a priest is in the pulpit, everyone sees the white collar and black cassock and says to himself, "Here comes another sermon. He's going to tell me that something I am doing is wrong, or I should do something better." If he says, "Turn to page so and so," the people say "Here he comes again." When I am the commentator, they know that somebody the same as they are is going to lead them. People accept me because I am *not* a priest—and I am participating in the Mass just as they are. They listen to me better than they would a priest because I am just like them.
>
> The priest says, "Don't do this, don't do that" in sermons. Sermons are fine, but how much good do they do? Isn't the example of even a few people going to do a lot more good than all the sermons, preaching and all the theories and everything else?

The layman as commentator inspires the congregation to fuller participation through emulation.

> People feel, "If my neighbor can do it, I can do it." Everybody knows a priest can do it, but if you are going to have lay participation you just have to have lay leadership.

> Before at Mass, it was only the priest. Now, seeing the regular layman, people feel they should participate more.
>
> In going through this Catholic education, we were always being preached at. At the same time, we were never given an opportunity to *do* something.
>
> The priest probably did a better job, probably made fewer mistakes. Maybe he gave better explanations of the Mass, but I think the people, over a period of time, actually appreciate the fact that one of our own is up there. Instead of the priest extending his own activities a little further, he is giving us more to do.

Something to Do

A visible sharing of the liturgy between priest and laity has definite effects on a parish. People are more vocal, as this book can testify. People become more vocal, it would seem, because now they have something to talk about, because now there is something which they can point to with pride as their own product. The liturgy is not their own product, of course, but the parish is. In the words of the commentators:

> Even though a priest might do it better technically, the advantage is in the attitude of the person in the pew. From day to day, from Sunday to Sunday, the overall impression—because a layman is the commentator—is that the congregation at large is taking part in the Mass. The priest may be our representative—but he is too remote.
>
> My enthusiasm for the thing, and my delight in it, is that it leads me closer to what the Mass should be. Lay participation is closer to the community offering the Mass, rather than having the one estate, the priesthood, and the other estate, the laity, operating on two different sides of the altar rail, each more or less inde-

> pendent with no rapport back and forth, with no community action. My delight and enthusiasm comes from the thought that this is the right idea. This is the people taking part in the Mass.
>
> We can't get away from the idea that the layman is the better representative of laymen than the priest. If the laity is to participate in the Mass, then a member of the community must participate. This is not jealousy or resentment, or any idea that we ought to regain some power from the clergy. Rather it's the idea that if the people are to participate, they ought to participate in the way appropriate to them. A representative of the people is the appropriate thing here. Therefore a lay commentator is what makes all the difference. I'd call it the ultimate in active participation in the Mass—lay commentators.

These are men speaking who have a deep sense of their own leadership, and as we will see later, who are looked upon by the parish with pride as being leaders. Such phenomena have some intriguing implications in many other areas, but certainly one should pause to consider that lay leadership of this kind might provide the key to militant Catholic leadership at a time when the Church needs more than ever to have all her members stand up and be counted for their faith. If I may speak as an observer, and all on my own for a moment, I must say that they have become much more identified with the Church. They are more responsible, more eager to undertake apostolic works; not all have been close to the Church, and some were almost total strangers before their involvement in participation.

Active participation *in the parish* has become a reality at St. Rose of Lima not because of the singular efforts of the priests, or the efforts of the laity who presumably got fed up with being left out (etc., etc.), but because of the efforts of both groups. As one man said, "I think the laity put it across finally. But, it was only because two priests insisted that this *had* to work, and looked for ways to make it work. Remember, you never thought of the lay commentator when you first started the singing." Actually, when that remark was made, I really had forgotten that fact. It was teamwork, a clergy-laity team, working together that won out. Successful teamwork in the ritual of the Mass has a way of extending itself successfully into the rest of the parish life:

> Lay people should have more voice in the Church. Not just at Mass, but in other things as well. A person should be made to feel a part of everything that goes on in the parish. Why not? We feel that we are part of everything that goes on in our own homes. I think this will bring people closer to the Church. Why shouldn't it? In the first place, it means they are willing to do little things they are asked to do. If they don't try for a voice, that means they are not interested. Take CFM, for instance. When I joined CFM, I had not done in five years—from the time I was out of school until I got married—the things I did in one year after I had joined CFM. This was simply because I knew I was *a part of things*. The same applies to the Church. If people are given a voice, they will respect it and love it.

> It's nice to say that this is the age of the layman, but there can be no age of the layman if he is not given anything to do. He must have some function in Church society, just as he does in secular society.

And More Knowledge

> My understanding of the Mass, through my participation as a commentator, has helped me to grasp the importance of the Mass.

Priests are apt to view the role of the lay commentator solely from the practical standpoint of helping the congregation to participate better. It is not unusual to label the exuberance and enthusiasm of commentators about their job as superficial. Such a degree of professional "snobbery" is unjustifiable, especially when we examine more deeply the reasons why these men appreciate their role so much. Those reasons are solidly grounded.

Commentating whetted their interest in the Mass. This happened in our parish *in spite of* the fact that many of the men were not able to read articles or books on the Mass. In view of the failure of many of our past efforts to generate an increased interest in the Mass, this personal success of lay commentating is all the more remarkable. The sacrificial action of oblation takes on new meaning for the men; it begins to be a living reality; they become more closely identified with Christ as his instruments:

> When I started narrating, only then did I begin to understand the various parts of the Mass, the various levels and stages of progression in the Mass.
>
> We've all gotten a better appreciation and understanding of the Mass.
>
> We have learned the Mass because we are narrating the Mass. Commentating has forced our attention on it. You learn more about the Mass when you are doing something.
>
> I am a lot more concerned with the meaning of the Mass. I so desire everyone in the congregation at Mass to desire it and feel it the way I do; so I try to put the greatest amount of feeling that I can in the reading. I want everybody there to share the same things that I'm experiencing.
>
> Being a narrator and learning more about the Mass was finding an outlet for my expression to give and get more appreciation. It is so important for us to give instead of just being blotters and soaking everything up

> —anything anybody throws at us. When you soak everything up, all you are is a sponge. That's even a better expression than a blotter. A blotter blots something and it is going to show back, even if it's gooey. But a sponge just soaks everything up. All you have to do if you are a sponge is lay there. You soak.
>
> I feel I am part of the congregation. At the same time, I am representing all the people. If the priest is a representative of Christ, what is the narrator? As far as I am concerned, he is a tool in the hands of the Lord to help the rest of the people. There is a lot of personal satisfaction in knowing that I am being used by God. I feel that when I read, God is flowing through this reading. I am merely using the talents and abilities which God has given me in the best way I can toward expressing Him. It seems God is trying to speak through me at this Mass, through the ordinary lay person, in a humble, quiet sort of way so that the people can in some way feel the spirit of the Mass.
>
> It does me good. I'm looked up to. People are depending on me. I get a great deal of satisfaction out of it, a great deal. It makes me feel really good that I am an instrument in leading others.
>
> It was something I appreciated being able to do, so there was satisfaction in it. It was something I thought was eminently worthwhile, so there was a sense of conviction that this was something good to be done.
>
> I feel this is the closest I could come to doing some duty in a priestly manner. This is a great accomplishment for me. I can't do anything better. When I get through with a Mass, I feel I have accomplished something. I wish I could do it more often.

Not to be overlooked would be the good influence upon the commentator's family. Without a doubt, the wife and children share the experience and feelings of the lay commentator.

> My boy thinks this is the greatest thing when we say, "This is daddy's Sunday." There isn't every wife or kid that can say "my husband," or "my daddy" does this. My wife thinks it is something terrific. Once in a while she knocks me because she says: "Here you are a commentator and what did you say?"

Does it seem strange that these men look forward to, appreciate, and place such a high importance on commentating? That's the way it is, so much so that when one of the commentators said, "I feel *sorry* for anybody who is not a narrator because I don't think until I started doing this that I ever appreciated the Mass," he stated the sentiments of all.

On the Other Hand

> At first it was kind of hard for me to get used to having a lay commentator. It seems as though when the priest is the commentator, it holds more meaning.

Not everyone sees the lay commentator in such a saving light. But these are the reactions of a minority group and range from opposition to tolerance to indifference. Some found the lay commentator hard to accept. A few objected outright. A small number preferred a priest, especially for reading the Scriptures:

> That's a priest's job and it should not be substituted or given to anyone else.

> I don't think it's good to have a lay commentator. It introduces a form of acting. The man is up there *reading* the Scripture, something off a paper, just like on the stage. When the priest reads the Scripture, he knows what he is reading. You ask a priest a question, he knows

> what he is talking about. The lay commentator probably could not answer. He'd probably say "Wait a minunte, I'll go call Father John." If you go to Church, you want it to be conducted by a *priest.*
>
> I told my neighbors about having a lay person narrate the Mass. They didn't like it at all. They said they didn't know how I could stand it every Sunday. I told them I didn't like it either, but I go because I have to go on Sundays anyway.
>
> I look up to the priest. If I hear the Epistle and Gospel from the priest, I like it much better. I believe the priest should have that honor.
>
> It's really a privilege giving this job to a lay person—but it was just too much for me at first.
>
> I think having the commentator is a good approach, having the layman guide the people along, help them learn the Mass. But I like the Gospel read by the priest.
>
> I enjoy the lay commentator better now, but if the priest would do it, it would add a little more feeling to it.

A few others commented in a parallel vein, not really objecting to the layman reading the Scriptures but preferring a priest. Some others looked upon the lay commentator from a more practical standpoint. They looked upon him in the light that he was helping the priest, "substituting for him."

Are Commentators Needed?

Some parishes have begun active participation without commentators and continue that way. Negative reactions from people, as we have seen, are in the minority—but there are a suprising number of priests who subscribe to the position that commentators are an unnecessary nuisance. Do people feel a need for a commentator? Here I think it's best to let them speak entirely on their own. There is so much wisdom in the following that any additional remarks would be ludicrous.

> A prompter is really necessary to put over a project such as active participation. You have to have someone to *coach* the people.
>
> When there is no commentator, and I get beside somebody who's going like the dickens, I'm lost.
>
> You've got to have a good leader who can sing, at each Mass—a forceful leader.
>
> If the Mass is to be an "undistractor" then it has to be led. You have to know what you are doing, when to respond. Once we had an all-school Mass—a Dialogue Mass. We freshmen were up in the balcony and we couldn't tell what was going on. They lost us completely. Then we had a retreat and we were down closer to the altar and we could at least *hear* the person who was leading. It was much better.
>
> The commentator has to be a leader. He starts you off but if you don't hear him after that, you kind of die away.
>
> The commentator should be *seen!!* Don't have him hidden behind the grill like a voice coming from the wilderness. That's part of the trouble at this one parish. The man who plays the organ says, "Page mumble, mumble." You don't hear it for one thing so it doesn't work. The commentator should direct the participation. The system at St. Rose is effective. There is no doubt about the commentator directing the congregation and the congregation responding. Any crowd can be directed and that's what a commentator does. You don't

have chaos. You don't have anarchy. You have a *directed* group, a group that is acting together because they are being led. Half the reasons why people don't participate, why they don't sing, is because they are not sure of themselves. They would be sure of themselves if they were directed, if they felt what they were doing was correct, if they knew that when they stood up they were *supposed* to be standing and so forth.

If there is somebody to help guide the people and keep them together, you fall into the spirit much better.

You have to be together to have it enjoyable, but if somebody starts a few syllables behind you, you're lost and they're probably lost, too.

I think it is an advantage to have these men there. They have told me things about the Mass I never knew before.

I don't understand most of what is going on at the altar so the commentator helps me.

A lot of people who come to Church don't even know what they come for. When a commentator is there he tells them and keeps them on their toes. It helps a person put his mind to God.

I think a lay person is fine. I don't even think that it is very important whether a priest or laymen does it—it's the *way* they lead the people that is important. They have to be able to get across to the people the idea of participation at Mass. They have to be able to communicate. I think a priest could do it just as well as a lay person. Whoever it is must be effective in his speaking.

I didn't even give it a thought. It's read and I listen to it the same as if the priest were doing it. I wouldn't even know the priest wasn't doing it. It's just that I know most of the voices now and I know it is not a priest. It doesn't bother me a bit. I don't think it makes any difference.

Definitely Preferred

It is good to know that he is a layman like yourself. It's like a part of you that brings a closeness between us all. Someone is guiding you without a pall of orders descending upon you.

Why do lay people prefer a layman as commentator to a priest? Why do they feel more at ease? What is responsible for this difference of attitude, and the different atmosphere created at Mass?

A layman is better because he is one of us. To me, the mere sight of a man dressed in street clothes in the role of commentator holds appeal. I think I stand for the average person in saying that.

When the priest was there, I had the feeling he was trying to teach us something. But when the layman got up there I thought now this guy learned it—maybe now we can learn it too.

I was going to say that having a priest there would put him again in the role of teacher and we would be the pupils. He's teaching us religion again all during the Mass, not only at the time of the sermon. Having a lay commentator up there—he isn't teaching us. He's *leading* us, and we are all doing it together. We are very important to the commentator and he is very important to us. We are on his level. We don't feel that he knows any more than we do. He's one of us. He has learned right along with us.

When a priest does it, it sounds more like an instruction. When a layman does it, the teaching tone disappears. When the Gospel is read by the layman, it's different. The priest has to do it, but coming from the

> layman, it loses the overtone of obligation. There *is* a different feeling there: I feel the lay commentator is speaking to me. When a priest talks, I know there is an instruction coming. The layman speaks for everybody, on behalf of everybody.
>
> I think when a priest reads the Epistle and the Gospel, he tends to preach it. When a layman does it, he does it with a little more feeling. A lot of priests get up there and rattle it off so fast you don't even know what he said.
>
> When the priest makes announcements, he makes them with authority, and there are a lot of people who resent this. Priests will pound on different points. The layman's approach is more subtle, more in keeping with our own train of thought.
>
> If the priest is commentating, you feel he's trying to *make* you do it. But with a layman, you yourself want to do it. It's better now.
>
> He's just an ordinary Joe like you or me. You feel more or less with him, that he is one of us. He is not ordering you around. You're more inclined to go along with him.
>
> We feel closer to the Mass, closer to God, closer to the Church when a layman is the commentator.

People see the position of lay commentator as a positive value to the whole community. Some indicated that as the *image* of the Church changes, their attitude toward the Church changes.

> It gives the whole congregation a better attitude toward the Church. Some of them may not admit it because of some old feeling they may have thinking a priest should be there, but actually in their hearts they all feel better if a layman is there. They realize the fact that the Church doesn't feel she is elevated too high above

the layman, that the layman is part of the Church. This makes us feel at home. If a priest did everything and the layman was kept out, he wouldn't have the same feeling toward the Church. It's really nice at St. Rose. That's not only my feeling. I've heard it from other people, many of whom were strangers to the parish. They said they were never at a Church that had such a Mass. It showed the Church wanted the public to take an interest in it. The only way you can get the public to take an interest is by giving them a part in it. If they had a part in it, it would even interest people who aren't taking a part. They would get interested in it just the same.

It gives us a feeling of being closer to the Mass and everything that is going on; in other words, it unifies. We feel more a part of the Mass because the commentator is one of us.

To me, the altar was some place where you can never go, because you can never quite reach it. There's something beautiful about being close to the altar. The few times that I got close there was a marvelous feeling. But to me the altar was always so out of reach—because we could never get as close as we would really like. The only times we ever got to go close to the altar were when we made our First Communion, when we graduated from grammar school, and then again when we graduated from high school. Just being close was perfectly breathtaking. If you had someone at the altar, it would seem like it was more in reach, taking away that attitude that people seem to have that it is a stage—the priest acts on the stage; you're in the audience and you're only there to watch. It's like going to the theatre. You can never get on the stage, you can never come in as close contact as you would like to the actors. If you have a lay commentator, it bridges the gap more than when we had a priest, because that seemed like just adding another player to the cast.

> It's much better to have a lay person as a commentator because it brings the priest closer to the congregation. It seems we are more closely related. If a priest were the commentator, it would be just another member of the clergy at the altar. It is better to have a lay person.
>
> The lay commentator is one of us as he is participating. It makes the layman feel better and more important to have some part, no matter how small.
>
> The more people that are involved, the better it is. It becomes more than just a one-man show. It becomes more effective for participation.
>
> Ordinarily the priest does everything for you. You don't have anything to do for yourself. The lay commentator is speaking for me; he bridges a gap between the priest and the lay person. The Church has tried to teach lay people to be lay apostles. With the people helping the priest along as far as the recited Mass goes, it seems the people get closer to the priest and seem to work right with him. This is what the Church is striving for—lay apostles. What better way for people to become lay apostles than by coming closer to God through the Mass?

What better way indeed? Such spontaneous and unrehearsed choices of words reveal many basic things. People draw sharp contrasts between priests and laymen; they are agonizingly conscious of the distance between themselves and the priest, or is it the Church? There is an immediacy, a closeness, between them and a lay commentator who is "part of us," "one of us," who is not "barking orders."

The lay commentator is not authoritarian, because he dares not be. For whatever reasons, the priest's manner is described as authoritarian: "will pound away at you," "ordering you around," "tends to preach it." Let no one think this description is appealing—"pall of orders descending upon you," "trying to teach us," and the list could go and on. The commentator, a layman, leads the laity to participation. He is not unlike the playing captain (and let no one confuse the playing captain with the coach). His team members "feel with him," because he keeps with "our own train of thought."

The commentator is linked more to the congregation; he helps the community fulfill their role. The layman who reads the Scriptures is somehow part of them, too. There is a quiet insistence underlying all this that the priest's job is to "celebrate Mass." The priest has his own liturgy, the Canon, the Eucharistic Sacrifice. The people share in this one Sacrifice too, but no one really confuses the roles here. The first joy of participation, and it is inextricably linked with the person of the lay commentator, is the sense of belonging, the welcome and acceptance in the Church, by the Church. This is something new, to most people at least.

Thus the commentator helps the congregation to participate, that is, to sense the real appropriateness of their presence at Mass. The commentator is the servant of the people—remember the meaning of the word "deacon"—and yet he is clearly one of the congregation, identified with them, an honored representative, an equal among equals. The dignity of the priest-president, and how telling that term of the Council is in the full context, is NOT to be an equal among equals. Otherwise he could be neither "priest" nor "president." But unless he has the loving assistance (or participation) of the community who has come together to offer Sacrifice and partake of the Sacrifice which is offered back to them, how can he be either?

It is fitting then that one of the congregation steps into the role of uniting them to the priest, or leading them, or helping them to participate. The differences between such statements are so miniscule that one wonders whether or not they really exist. An equal should lead equals. When the priest steps into the functions of the people, he ceases to be "priest" in the first sense that he became priest. The role of commentator ceases to be commentator, too. The priest in this role has become a new entity, and there is no word for him.

Summarily, people feel "with" the layman commentator. His presence encourages them to imitate his example, and join in. The honor which the parish accords these men is great. They become a source of other commentators. When Pope Pius XII said, "You are the Church," he expressed a reality which takes on flesh and blood in the liturgy celebrated in this fashion for here there is a sensible closeness to the Church, to Christ the Priest; there is representation, there is sharing, there is the union of our Baptismal promises, the love of our one Eucharist. Perhaps the view of the value of the layman as commentator for the person in the pew is best summarized in this brief exchange—

> "It's really bringing the Mass down to *us*."
> "No it's not—it's bringing us up to the *Mass*."
> "It's ours. It's more a *sharing* . . ."

[9]
Personal Reflections

ARTICLE 21 of the Constitution on the Sacred Liturgy, the decree of April, 1964 by our American bishops, and the September 26, 1964 *Instructio* from Rome, give us the guidelines for the process of change and renewal in our liturgy. Needless to say, great numbers of interested people have been speculating on the many ways of "changing" our Eucharist, especially: speculation is challenging and carries its own rewards within it. While our own speculation has led us to a deeper understanding and appreciation of the Mass, we do not presume to lay down any definitive suggestions. Some things which the American Church is now doing for the first time as a body are exciting and encouraging; but they are by their very nature *temporary* steps, and one presumes that honest and respectful criticism of how effective they are in helping the People of God to pray better and more rewardingly will be welcomed.

Therefore, when we suggest changes, our intention is not to sway the hierarchy but rather to confront the Church—clergy and laity—with propositions for thoughtful consideration and discussion. Someone should undertake a study parallel to this one on the reactions of the laity to these suggested changes—it would be of more than passing interest.

We will prescind in this examination from an intellectual examination of the content and order of prayers, and from ideological reflections on *what* the Mass is supposed to be, etc. These changes are suggested from our own experience of the liturgy; it has come to mean many things to us, oftentimes in spite of the rite itself.

From a psychological point of view, the Mass is an artistic masterpiece. Glance at the prayers of preparation, the entrance hymn, the prayers of sorrow, mercy, praise, petition and instruction, all interspersed with songs, which are prayers themselves and rewarding in other areas of human experience. It would be difficult to improve on this psychological structure of the preliminary prayers related to the Eucharistic Sacrifice proper.

But does the layman experience the impact of this dramatic conception? Priests may really and truly experience the worship of God in the Mass even as it now stands, stumbling over the meaning of some phrases perhaps, but generally speaking *enjoying* the celebration of Mass and the elevating, personal satisfaction which comes from something done with a deep personal involvement. But the Mass is not the worship of the priest alone. It's the worship of the Body of Christ, the entire Body; it's the worship of all the faithful in the parish. Really, though, is it the worship of the *whole* parish? or is it simply the prayerful activity of the priests and a few elite?

The majority of Catholics will still insist that they pray each in his own way in the surroundings of the Mass. One man expressed it:

> I really pray and get lost in my prayers. I don't participate. I don't know what's going on at the altar.

No one is questioning the efficacy of the Mass *ex opere operato,* nor is anyone seeking to discredit the minimum requirements of attention and intention dictated by moral theology for the fulfillment of the Sunday obligation and some sharing of the fruits of the Mass. But the question still stands: *does* the ordinary layman experience sacrificial worship?

We must abandon the practice of a too mechanistic concept of the outpouring of grace in the Mass, and try to grasp the Mass in a more vital way. What are the obstacles present in the ritual presentation of the Mass that prevent people from appreciating, understanding and sharing more deeply in the riches of the worship of the Church? Technical or ritual perfection cannot guarantee that the non-performing members of the community *benefit* from the rite as persons. Granted that there is a tremendous outpouring of grace anyway—but one might just as well object that grace is outpoured in spite of the rite, not because of it and hand-in-hand *with* it.

In any communication, we have two viewpoints—one, the giver's and the other, the receiver's. Put in another way—one, the teacher; the other, the student. The qualifications required of a teacher naturally will be different from what is required of the students.

The teacher is concerned with what is given and how that is to be presented; but he cannot entirely ignore the student. The student will receive the matter presented according to the manner in which he is capable of receiving it. Possibilities recommended will stem from the study of the recipients' manner of receiving the communication. From this viewpoint, we will recommend to the "teacher" a change in content or approach of presentation more attuned to the recipients' capacity.

Sociological and psychological factors are of importance and are not to be ignored in our study of the Mass. The supernatural transforms the natural. The supernatural works after the manner of the natural only in a higher way—a supernatural elevation and transformation of man. The fruits and graces of the Mass come to us not in some magical or mechanical way, but pattern themselves after the manner of man.

We dare to question respectfully the ritual presentation of the Sacrifice of the Mass as it is now executed in the non-essential prayers, gestures, ceremonies and so forth. We question the value of some accidentals, some externals, some recent changes. Thus we have sought to discover the living experience of the laity at Mass. Our study together with the recommendations of possible changes centers around the Sunday Community Mass. We realize our recommendations can only bear a personal value. Final decisions belong to the hierarchy.

From the general background of the great number of interviews we had, we present the following possible ideas that would make the Mass more meaningful for the people.

Point One

The basic psychology of the Mass is attuned to man's nature. The Proper of the Mass changes, the Ordinary generally remains the same. Man searches for stability. He tires of sameness and seeks to avoid the boredom of routine through refreshing change. The rigid structure of the Ordinary of the Mass satisfies man's need for security. The changeable parts of the Mass, the Proper, satisfy his desire for change. Looking at it from an intellectual point of view, we find the Mass structured in this way.

Let us look at the Mass experientially from the viewpoint of the people. How do they see the Mass? To them, practically speaking, it is always the same, Sunday after Sunday. They know the Gospel changes; sometimes the color of the vestments change; but for all practical purposes, for the majority of Catholics who attend Mass on Sunday, the Mass on one Sunday seems entirely similar to the Mass on the previous Sunday. A statement from an interview illustrates this point:

> You get tired of the same thing over and over again.

The student of the Mass can appreciate the present variations in the Mass much more than the ordinary Catholic. *Reading* the Proper in the Missal doesn't come close to fulfilling the need for experiential change. The ordinary Catholic must somehow experience the joy that comes from the break of the boredom of routine. He does not experience the refreshment of change. Some change ought to be made in the Mass that would help him to enjoy the Mass more . . . experience a dramatic variation in the Mass every Sunday. The Mass would then become more true to life. Life is in a constant state of flux, a constant state of change. It is not rigid, not stereotyped. All growth involves change, especially spiritual growth. This is not a question of novelty. This is life.

The Mass must be offered so that the generality of Catholics would experience refreshment or change at the same time that they would find security and stability in the Mass.

Point Two

As much as priests may appreciate the High Mass, we must all face the fact that Solemn or Simple, High Mass fails to convey, to the majority of Catholics, any solemnity. They may enjoy and appreciate the High Mass on special occasions, Christmas, Easter, Forty Hours Devotion, the presence of a high dignitary, anniversaries—but otherwise they want no part of it. We all witness the fact that the majority of Catholics seek to escape the High Mass in any Church, regardless of the excellence of the choir. Watch the faces and catch the comments of Catholics when they walk into Church and see six candles lit on the altar. This is not an isolated few, but the majority. We can question why. Is the fault altogether in the people? Perhaps there is some defect in the ritual that needs to be remedied.

At the same time, we find a near unanimous approval on the part of the people for singing. People enjoy singing in Church. They experience many beneficial effects from it. Many even found it easier to sing the Latin in preference to saying it. How to reconcile these facts?

Three clinical facts are evident from the interviews:

1. People enjoy and desire singing in Church.
2. They experience a greater facility of singing the Latin over saying it.
3. They reject the Solemn High Mass or High Mass.

We do not need to prove the thesis that singing should be part of Sunday worship. It is natural to sing. People want to sing. Song was part of the ancient liturgy of the Temple. Christ sang at the Last Supper with the Apostles. Tradition and history of all people show that singing is part of man's worship of God. Man worships God through song.

Apart from the High Mass, what music do Catholics hear in Church on Sunday? A soloist, organ interludes, occasionally a children's choir singing hymns . . . mostly dead silence. Only in a few parishes in our particular Archdiocese is there congregational singing on Sundays, even in those parishes with a certain amount of participation at Mass. The ordinary Catholic's experiential worship is without song. It is contrary to nature, to tradition. Before major changes are envisioned or demanded for the Mass, let us first restore singing to the Sunday worship of every Catholic. Singing must be restored to Sunday worship, but not the singing of the High Mass as we know it.

Point Three

Restore some of the prayers of the Mass to their original function. For example: the Introit prayer was meant as an entrance song. It was hardly meant to be said by the celebrant in the fashion as it is said in our day and read by the people from their Sunday Missals as they are following the priest. It was meant as an entrance song, not an entrance prayer. Similarly, other prayers ought to be restored to their original function.

Point Four

The Mass ought to radiate international, national, diocesan and parochial characteristics. Uniformity can be contrary to nature. God did not impose uniformity on his rational creatures. Witness the uniqueness of each individual: the even greater uniqueness among the angelic hosts. Let the worship of each nation differ from every other nation. Let each diocese show diversity: let every parish radiate an individual character in its worship to God. All of this should remain rooted in a solid, Catholic, international structure, uniformity in essentials, diversity in some incidentals. Again, in the present Mass, the Catholic character is self-evident, but diversity is lacking.

Point Five

Members of the community must more fully participate in the Sacrifice of the Mass to immerse the community more experientially into the Sacrifice of the Mass. The priest represents Christ, and he represents the people—the mediator between God and man—one with God and one with man—a member of the community, the parish for whom he offers the Sacrifice of the Mass. But the people do not look upon the priest as a member of the community, but rather as set apart from it, coming from elsewhere to the community, never really becoming a part of it. This separation of the priest from the people exists in the minds of the people. We know that there is a division canonically speaking between a priest and the laity and rightly so. But the gulf exists so much so that he is not even looked upon as part of the community. Why this should so exist we will leave to others to discover. The fact that it does is a reality.

It is not fair in this and other parallel cases to scapegoat past generations of clergy for present realities. We must face the fact of changing rather than excuse ourselves by blaming others. For a fuller participation in the Mass, a deeper participation, a member of the community who is so regarded must plunge the rest of the community into a deeper celebration of the Mass. Thus, it becomes a community offering themselves to God *through* the Mass, *in* the Mass.

The position of lay commentators at Mass conveys publicly and symbolically the participation of the community in the Sacrifice of the Mass. Lay commentators bridge a gap between priests and people. Somehow, in the minds of the people, he draws them closer to the priest and makes them one with the priest. Clericalizing the lay commentator or lay representative through minor orders will destroy their tremendous symbolic value! In addition, lay representatives ought to perform some other, additional functions for the entire community now reserved to the ordained priest.

Point Six

People express a deep desire to understand the Mass, to know what is going on, and why. Everyone has expressed this thought with sincerity, with force, with more conviction than any other. Somehow, the very celebration of the liturgy, of the Mass, must quench this deep thirst for understanding of the Mass without added effort. The Mass as it is celebrated on Sunday must satisfy their deeper yearning for a fuller knowledge and understanding of the Mass. We cannot rely on personal reading, discussion clubs, etc., to satisfy this need. Through the Mass, we must teach, inspire, satisfy the basic thirst for knowledge of the Mass. We must sanctify the people through our Sunday worship. In reality, the present manner of celebrating Mass does not quench their thirst for understanding the Mass.

Point Seven

In the Mass, there is a division of function among individuals which the liturgy postulates but is not experientially clear-cut. The priest has his role, the people theirs, the altar boys, choir, lay commentator, etc., no one absorbing one another's role.

Point Eight

A comment or two would be in order on the use of the Latin and the vernacular. We do not necessarily have to draw battle lines between the two. There is no doubt about the desire of the people craving a deeper understanding of the Mass, to understand as they participate. At the same time, there is the wish to retain something that would carry back to their past.

Most find no objection to saying Deo Gratias, Et cum spiritu tuo, Gloria tibi Domine in Latin, but they react strongly against saying the Gloria, or the Credo and similar prayers in Latin. Nor does it make much difference to most people if the priest says, for example, the Canon in Latin. As a matter of fact, most people prefer it. I think this is an accurate representation of what the people expressed of those I interviewed.

Point Nine

Many people found it very beneficial for the congregation to join in the very language of the minister, whether it be in Latin or the vernacular. It was very effective, very meaningful. It seemed to convey depth participation in the sacrificial action of the Mass.

The Mass in Transition

A. ENTRANCE SONG—THE ORIGINAL FUNCTION OF THE INTROIT

In the present day, hardly anyone experiences it as an entrance song. In the beginning, everyone sang it. Later only trained choirs sang it. Today, it is only read at the Masses that the majority of Catholics attend.

Does singing it in Latin or English even by a trained schola convey the idea of an entrance song to the people? Not at all. Besides, how many trained scholas are there in your diocese? How many groups even psalm-tone the Introit? If it cannot be done even at one Mass after all the effort made, how can it be done for all the Masses? Even if this were possible, the singing of the Introit falls short of the dramatic impact an entrance hymn should have.

Therefore, we begin each Mass with the singing of a popular hymn, fulfilling the psychological intent of the Introit, but not in the present day words of it. Perhaps later, antiphonal psalm singing may be introduced, but at present, the singing of a popular hymn best unifies the congregation with a spirit of joy. "With joy we will go unto the altar of God."

This parallels entrance experiences in our everyday lives—applauding at the entrance of a guest to a dining room; singing, for example, the National Anthem at the beginning of public functions. Why not a parallel entrance for Christ?

What is to be done with the present Introit? Eliminate it—or let it be read by the priest or a lay minister as his opening prayer of the Mass, or employ it in some fashion as a popular antiphon.

We feel no particular aversion for keeping the prayers at the foot of the Altar, including the priest's Confiteor. One might view these rather as a necessity, looking at the human weakness of priests and the importance we now place on the singing of an Entrance hymn. In the light of the practical inclination of the clergy to rush, to cut corners, if the Prayers at the Foot of the Altar were eliminated, the Entrance Song would tend to be anticipated, shortened or hurried. This way, if the priest has something to do at that particular moment, the Entrance hymn can be sung by the people in a leisurely, devout manner. After a number of years when the singing of an Entrance hymn becomes part and parcel of every community Mass, the transition towards the elimination of those prayers can be made. The priest could then join the congregation in singing the Entrance hymn. We would like to give the priest something to do while the Church ecclimatizes itself to the singing of an Entrance hymn at all the Masses in all churches.

The prayers at the foot of the altar should clearly indicate that they are the prayers of the priest and his altar ministers, and not the priest and the congregation.

B. SERVICE OF SORROW

The preparation of the priest needs to be much more thorough than that of the people, unique in its fashion because he is preparing to represent Christ. The present prayers at the foot of the altar may be retained for the priest and his ministers as their personal preparation of sorrow. A clear-cut distinction should be drawn between a preparation of the priests and his ministers at the altar and the preparation of the people.

For the people, the Service of Sorrow begins immediately after the singing of the entrance hymn. A lay commentator announces an examination of conscience for the people, focusing attention on the past week. After a fifteen second pause or so for examination, the lay commentator intones the Act of Contrition said publicly by the entire congregation. A choice must be made between saying the Act of Contrition or the Confiteor. The picture presented by the Confiteor is magnificent, but lacks psychosomatic overtones and association of sorrow for sin. Few laymen will ever be able to say the Confiteor, even in English, with a real personal meaning of sorrow. Sorrow for sin is a very intensely personal thing, yet this is not conveyed to him through this prayer. The Act of Contrition aptly awakens our experience of sorrow and recalls sentiments of sorrow associated with confession. This prayer may vary from nation to nation depending on the prevalent prayer form of sorrow in the country. We can readily grasp the value of saying a prayer that aims at eliciting a perfect Act of Contrition for sin. Surely the mad scramble through the Prayers at the Foot of the Altar hardly generates any real act of sorrow. The minds of the people need to be focused sharply on the Act of Contrition. This prayer above all must be a prayer in the language of the people. One cannot express sorrow through the parroting of words in a foreign tongue, but through a familiar formula of contrition.

The priest closes the Service of Sorrow, standing at the altar facing the people, chanting the ancient formula of general absolution, "Misereatur and Indulgentiam" in English. The people answer "Amen" to both.

C. KYRIE

Having reconciled themselves with God through the cleansing action of sorrow, both the priest and the people join together in prayer through the interaction of the Kyrie, addressed to the Trinity. People know what it means, or can easily learn. The Kyrie may be sung or said alternately between the priest, people and choir, or priest and the people.

D. GLORIA

The Mass not only must instruct us in the doctrine of Christ, faith and morals, but also must teach us how to pray, through a painless process, as one put it, "in service training" —learning by doing.

Three prayers in particular serve as models of different types of prayer, absent from the lives of many Catholics: Act of Contrition, Gloria, Credo. A fourth can be added: Domine, non sum dignus. Sentiments of sorrow, praise, adoration, thanksgiving, faith, humility, are all expressed. Prayers of petition need not be taught the people. They know how to do that quite well. Almost without exception, the people objected to saying these prayers in Latin. It is very understandable—they are the prayers of the people.

The Gloria is a beautiful composition of ejaculatory prayer. There can be very great value in having the people say it Sunday after Sunday. It synopsizes the Mass—gems of praise, thoughts of adoration, expressions people could memorize easily without added effort by reason of their regular attendance at Mass. These models of prayer memorized by the people in time would perfect the prayer of all people.

The singing or saying of the Gloria and Credo in Latin was of little or no value to most people. It was very difficult for most people to learn even to pronounce the Latin words, let alone know the meaning. Most people objected to saying the Gloria and Credo in Latin. Why? Simply this: They knew the Our Father in English from memory, thus they had a general conception of the prayer when they were saying it in Latin. Perhaps there was a rather accurate picture once they have memorized the Latin, but when they said the Gloria in Latin, they used Latin words without a corresponding reference in English. There was a memory code for understanding the one and not the other. However, the principal reason for reciting the Gloria in English is the memorization through constant use of the ejaculatory phrases. People will learn to praise God by praising him.

Sometime in abuses, we can detect true estimate of values or accurate feelings. Why were the Gloria and Credo cut short in singing in the past and still are cut short? Boring; makes the Mass drag; there is little prayer value to having the Gloria and Credo dragged out in song; singing of the Gloria and Credo lengthens the Mass without sufficient spiritual compensation for the people. There would be two exceptions to this: the singing of the Gloria on Holy Thursday and Holy Saturday.

E. RESPONSES

I am inclined to recommend the singing in Latin of all the responses because of the ease with which they can be made. However, the three groups of people interviewed who witnessed a demonstration of the Mass as recommended, did not feel comfortable with the "sandwiching" in of Latin responses if the Gloria, Collect, Epistle, Gospel, Credo and Post Communion were said in English. Therefore it seems to be better if the responses are all sung and retained in the Latin—beginning with the responses of the Preface up to and including the "Pax Domini sit semper vobiscum." The others could be in English.

Eventually everyone may learn the meaning because they are so short. People prefer singing them. It seems easier to sing Latin in unison in comparison to saying it. People feel a greater solemnity, beauty, sacredness. Song forces people to sing together. Music adds unity and order to participation.

F. COLLECT

Restore the original privilege of the Bishop to compose this prayer. Perhaps within certain limitations in a certain framework, this privilege could be extended to each celebrant. There are occasions when the Ordinary asks for special prayers for special intentions. Why not allow the Ordinary to make the intention a Collect prayer? The Collect could, of course, incorporate intentions more attuned to contemporary needs and problems. For example, problems of segregation, social problems, economic problems, divorce, delinquency, Catholic Action. Obviously, the Collect ought to be said in English for the fullest effect.

G. SERVICE OF INSTRUCTION

Epistle. A solemn announcement of the Epistle parallel to the present-day Gospel announcement is made. The Epistle is then read in the vernacular by a lay lector. At the end of the Epistle, all answer "Thanks be to God." Singing the Epistle in Latin or English serves no practical purpose—an investment of time and effort without proportionate advantage. Such parts that prolong the Mass without adding meaning to it should be eliminated. The ancient chants—Gradual, Alleluia, Tract—are beautiful when rendered properly, but they are more like a museum piece, like a work of art of a master in an art gallery, to be admired, imitated, but out of place in the home of the ordinary Catholic. Such ancient chants seem to be out of place in our ordinary Sunday worship. They can serve as models, as inspiration for contemporary works.

The reading of the Epistle likewise provides an occasion for a lay member of the community to take a more active part in the Mass. As the layman reads the Epistle the congregation sits and listens to his words, including the celebrant. After the congregation answers "Thanks be to God" to the Epistle, a short pause for reflection should follow. Perhaps a synoptic statement of a sentence or two about the Epistle after it is read would be very advantageous for such reflection. It should be limited to thirty seconds, preferably against a background of organ or choir music.

Gospel. "Munda Cor," the prayer of preparation for the Gospel should be said by the lector of the Gospel and should differ from the prayer said by the congregation.

The present prayer, "Munda cor meum," is suitable for the announcer of the Gospel. A short community prayer parallel to the present "Munda cor" may be said by the community, either together or silently, with this difference: the prayer for the congregation would ask for the grace to hear the word of God, understand it and witness it to others in our daily lives through works of Catholic Action. The reader of the Gospel requests a blessing from the celebrant that he may worthily announce the Gospel. I would like to see the reading of the Gospel restored to the layman, someone in addition to the lay lector of the Epistle. The present solemn announcement of the Gospel would be retained. At the end of the Gospel, all people of the congregation would answer "Praise be to You, O Christ." A short pause for reflection on the Gospel follows.

A sermon should have a maximum time limit and there should be a prohibition of all announcements at this time. The temptation is too great for any priest to drag out the announcements on pet projects, parish or otherwise.

H. THE CREED

A fitting transition prayer from prayers of preparation to the Sacrifice proper, this Act of Faith should be made with understanding. The people should know what they are assenting to; thus, the Creed should be said in the vernacular together with the priest. Similar to the Gloria, the singing of the Creed prolongs the Mass without adding meaning to it, especially when it is sung in Latin. If you want to say, "I believe," you have to use expressions that are meaningful, otherwise you are merely mouthing words.

I. THE OFFERTORY

The Offertory action of the Mass opens with the words of the priest "The Lord be with you." "Let us pray." Fittingly sung, these encompass the whole prayerful action of the Offertory ending with the "Amen" of the Secret prayer. At the Offertory, we again restore an original function of the Offertory antiphon. It was sung while gifts were brought to the altar. We eliminate the present day Offertory antiphon and substitute an Offertory hymn sung by the congregation.

During the Offertory of the Mass, we have another occasion to plunge the community deeper into the Mass through a lay representative. The offering of the bread and wine, a priestly function now performed by an ordained minister, can be performed by a lay representative. A layman, named as a lay representative of the community, can go to the altar, offer the bread, say the prayer alone in the vernacular or in conjunction with the priest. Then another lay representative, or the same one, alone or again in conjunction with the priest, offers the wine. Preferably, the offering should be made only by the lay representative for sharper significance. The community would offer itself to the fullest extent through the offering of the bread and wine, the fruits of mankind. No more can human nature do. Then it is that Christ in the person of the priest takes the gifts that mankind gives and changes them into the Body and Blood of Christ. The consecratory power of the priest would stand out in greater clarity.

A lay representative of the community speaks for the community as the community gives itself in the offering of the bread and wine—its work, its joys, its sufferings. It can offer no more. But the offering remains valueless by comparison until the consecratory action of the priest takes place, transforming them into the Body and Blood of Christ, offering them to God the Father. Such an Offertory action would be a living sign clearly showing the Offertory action of the participation of the community and the role of the priest with precise clarity. We need not search far for a theological justification. We all share in the priesthood of Christ through the sacraments of Baptism and Confirmation. As Congar says: [1]

> Baptismal consecration makes lay people liturgical persons, members of God's people as distinct from non-consecrated people who are not God's people.

The liturgical functions of the priest can be shared with a number of people. Great numbers of men would become more active in the Mass in a very meaningful way. There would follow a very forceful effect on the participants in the whole

[1] Yves Congar, O.P., *Laity, Church and World* (Baltimore, Md.: Helicon, 1960), p. 79.

community. Of the Offertory prayers, only the two said by the layman would be said in the vernacular. Other prayers may remain in Latin.

We can close the Offertory action of the Mass with the Secret prayer sung by the celebrant and the "Amen" sung by the congregation. In this manner, community participation in the Offertory would be two-fold, through the Offertory hymn sung by the congregation and by the offering of the bread and wine by the lay representative.

J. THE CANON

We open and close the Canon by singing the two most beautiful melodies of our liturgy, the Preface and the Our Father. The people join the priest in the singing of the Sanctus in English. The entire Canon will be said in Latin by the priest alone. The silence of the Canon will be broken by mementos of the living and dead made by the lay representative. The words of Consecration should be said in a loud tone of voice by the celebrant.

Such a solemn break in the silence of the Canon effectively draws the attention of the entire congregation to the Consecratory action on the Altar. All eyes would be focused on the Altar rather than as now, buried in their hands, or in their prayerbooks. The Canon of the Mass closes with the great "Amen" sung by the people.

We recommend the formulation of a Canon that the laity can read. The Canon of the minister is not totally fitting in all its respects, for the laity. Let us go back to another prayer mentioned earlier, the "Munda cor meum." In a parallel way, the Canon for the laity should closely follow the prayers of the priest, perhaps even using identical words, but in a manner more expressive of the role of the community in the action of the Mass, accurately delineating the laity's role as members of the Mystical Body in the offering of the Sacrifice of the Mass. Recasting of the Canon would be of importance to delineate the different role of the priest consecrator and the people participants, so clearly that it would be self evident for the majority of people.[2]

The most fitting prayer in preparation for the Sacrificial banquet is the Our Father jointly sung by priest and congregation. We can sharply differentiate the priest's prayer and the people's prayer of preparation for Holy Communion. It can be distinct from one another. The singing of the Agnus Dei by the congregation can be their sole preparatory prayer. It may be sung in Latin. In addition, a short prayer for the community can be composed from the priest's three prayers of preparation; however, it may be better to have an announcement by the commentator to focus our attention on the reception of Holy Communion by the priest and people. The acclamation "Ecce Agnus Dei," and the "Domine non sum dignus" dramatically focus the attention of the people on their reception of Holy Communion.

If the people had a choice of one prayer in the Mass to be said in the vernacular, they would choose, I am sure, this prayer: "Behold the Lamb of God. Behold Him Who takes away the sins of the world. Lord, I am not worthy, etc." The saying of this prayer in Latin raised more objections from the people than any other prayer.

[2] Following the Mass by reading the missal confuses rather than clarifies this point. Some of the prayers do not fit the layman nor does the present Mass of active participation sharply define the role of each. In the Mystical Body, each member plays a different role, so too in the Mass this ought to be self-evident. For a layman to read, "Cleanse my heart that I might worthily announce the Gospel" surely does not focus the layman's attention on the sentiments he should have for the hearing of the words of the Gospel. As in the Mystical Body, there is a diversity of function, so the Mass should symbolize and express the different roles.

K. COMMUNION ANTIPHON

We restore this antiphon to its original purpose—sung while all the people receive Holy Communion. A popular Eucharistic hymn would be a worthwhile substitute for the present Communion antiphon. A rapid distribution of Communion should take place with the help of married deacons.

Holy Communion would be received in the following manner: The priest or deacon would place the Host in the person's left hand. The person would then take the Sacred Host with his right hand and receive Him, or the person can take the Host immediately from the paten. The present manner of receiving the Host makes many people tense, nervous, self-conscious about opening their mouth at the Altar—an observation every priest can easily make. I can recall in my own life, in my youth, even as a seminarian in the major seminary, how self-conscious I was about opening my mouth, cleanliness of my teeth, position of my tongue and so forth. I have come to realize that I was not unique in this self-consciousness but very many people feel this way, even those who frequent the Sacraments often. How much more true this is of people who do not receive Holy Communion frequently, who go once a year, perhaps on rare occasions, people who have not received for many years. Perhaps this is one of the factors that keeps some people from more frequent reception of Holy Communion. Even if it were not so, it would be of value to eliminate any atmosphere which causes people to feel ill at ease when receiving Christ. Any form of anxiety can only detract or distract a person's concentration on the reception of Christ in Holy Communion. I recommend an added factor for consideration. In a way we are dealing with forms of communication, the ritual of communicating spiritual realities. A child is fed, an adult feeds himself. Would we not be communicating a more adult approach to Holy Communion if each fed himself with the Sacred Body? Was it not this way that the Apostles received their first Holy Communion?

The present Communion antiphon should either be omitted or be the first prayer of the priest's ablutions.

L. The remainder of the Mass remains the same (except to be said entirely in the vernacular) up to and including the priest's blessing. The priest's blessing should be chanted rather than said in a hurried fashion.

Immediately after the priest's blessing there is occasion for some quick announcements, if any, to be made by a lay representative.

It would be good for the priest to listen to these announcements made by the layman. More than likely, they would concern lay Catholic Action and lay parochial activities. Making these announcements at this time of the Mass tends to shorten them rather than lengthen them as they usually would be at the time of the sermon. We are all familiar with how sometimes the announcements constitute a sermon, frequently necessitating rushing through the Mass from that point.

M. After the announcements are made, the last Gospel should be omitted. At this time, the congregation sings a closing hymn. It would be a more fitting ending if the priest and the congregation sang the hymn together. The present last Gospel card can contain the hymn that would be sung.

This then, is the Sunday Community Mass, Sunday worship of mature adult Christians, as we conceive it. Christians should be able to perform actions for themselves rather than rely on others for their performance. These possible changes combine the best features of the present Recited Mass and the Sung Mass for a full community participation. Such a ritual gives a greater participation to the laymen, entitling them to an official status—at least to many of them, and of its very nature, a greater identification with the Church. It leads men to identify themselves more closely with the things of God.

[Appendix I]

What They Thought

A PUBLIC invitation was extended to all parishioners to participate in the program. Many were approached personally to set up gatherings in their homes. It was suggested that the host couple or individual invite six to eight people, whomever they desired. A good cross-section of parishioners was interviewed. I attended all the gatherings.

People knew in advance only the general discussion topic —Active Participation as You Have Experienced It at St. Rose of Lima Parish. No specific questions were asked. The general topic was announced. Everyone felt free to express themselves on the topic whenever they chose. No one was pressured to speak. Eventually everyone became involved in the conversation. General topics treated in this book were covered adequately without any further questioning on the moderator's part, with the exception of their views on the subject of the lay commentators and evaluation of the meeting at the very end.

The moderator attempted to place himself in their position applying the techniques of group counseling as explained by Rev. Charles Curran in his book. *Counseling In Catholic Life and Education,* Chapter XVII, pages 367-406.

The meeting was rather loosely structured; but an important part of the moderator's role was to recognize and reflect the feelings expressed, yet in no way to act the part of a teacher. Near the end of a few meetings, I switched from the role of one who was seeking to learn and understand to the role of teacher. The results were unfavorable as far as rapport was concerned between priest and people. People did not seem to like this and preferred that I stay in the role I had chosen for the evening. The counseling technique for group discussion is a very successful way of approaching people.

Everyone enjoyed the evening. All look forward to another similar discussion on this or other topics in a parallel way. It's a key that can unlock many doors. People felt honored to be asked for their opinions.

Let us evaluate the meeting in terms of the very language of the people. Of what were they most appreciative? Informal atmosphere, the atmosphere of acceptance.

> It's been very informal. It gave me a feeling of letting off steam. You listened to what we had to say. I enjoyed it. I felt you wouldn't get sore if I really told you what I felt. I thought it was helpful.
>
> I spoke among my type of people. I didn't have to be afraid to say this or that.

A very common reflection was:

> I've learned a lot. I thoroughly enjoyed it.

It was a help to people to discover that others felt the same way.

> I thought I was the only one who felt my way and now I know there are others. It gave me an outlet for my feelings.
>
> I found that I wasn't the only one who had different opinions on the way things should be in the Church.
>
> I like to hear what other people think.
>
> I enjoyed it and it's good to hear other people's point of view and to know that they think along similar lines.
>
> I find that this is a very pleasant thing—to hear the opinions of others.

Although the evening was not structured for teaching, people seemed to learn much from one another: thus, statements such as—"I have learned something from this"—"I have learned a lot that I didn't know when I came in"—were spoken frequently. A change of attitude toward the priest occurred. It created an atmosphere where people now feel more at ease in coming to a priest. It broke down a barrier.

> Anything that can be done to change my attitude toward the Church is good. I felt it was too stiff and formal; that I had to learn everything that was going on in order to become a part of the setup. This was a kind of imposed thing that I had no way of changing or talking about. It was supposed to be done this way and there was no questioning it. If nothing, this evening has shown me that I can express myself freely. What comes of it is another story. At least I've had an opportunity to talk about some of my feelings.

A change of attitude toward the priest seems to be very significant.

> There ought to be an effort made toward creating an atmosphere for those of us who do not have much know-how in the ways of the Church. I now feel more at ease in coming to a priest and asking questions about the Church. The thing that happened here this evening is that a barrier has been broken down between you and myself. Now I feel I can speak to you more freely about questions on my mind. Tonight was of great value to me in the sense that I have an entirely different feeling about you as a person and a priest. Now I can talk to you about anything. While you stepped out, I was telling the group that I have known you for ten years, but there always has been kind of a block between us. We talked about generalities but I never got close to you in any way. We've never gotten into anything controversial because of many fears on my part.
>
> Any opportunity where a lay person can get together on

intimate terms with the priest is always good. It is instilled throughout your life that a priest is a man of God. You owe him a certain respect. He is so much above you. You never attribute to him the same fears, passions that you have. In this setting, you are more one of us. I do feel much warmer now towards you than I have in the past. I'm still going to have a great love and respect for you as a priest, but at the same time I find we can love you as a man after this. Before, we respected you because it was required by reason of what you are, not because you earned it.

I'm sure you would go a lot further in reaching people on a much more relaxed and informal basis. I am even more enthused about going to Church now than I have been, if this is possible, and it is possible because of this evening's session. There should be more opportunities where the priest can meet more informally with people.

This puts life back into the Church. The impressions that most of us have about the Church are its stiffness, its unquestionability. Not that we want to break this down; there is a certain sense of security in that. There has not been enough thought put into taking the routine out of going to Church and putting things in such a way that people would understand better and maybe become a part of the Church. I think, as we keep preaching democracy, keep preaching participation, it could become a mockery if this is all one-sided, if we don't have an opportunity to convey our feelings, that we don't get to feel "Gee, I was part of this, or we discussed this." I am a part of it. This is the true meaning of democracy. As soon as it gets dictatorial then we're lost. I do want it to be flexible enough to fit my needs, for the Church to be attuned to and aware of my needs. If the Church gives this feeling of rigidity, that there is no opportunity for change, or even to voice an opinion, you're going to lose those people who can't meet the

> rules or laws that were set centuries ago for a set of situations that took place at that time.
>
> This is completely different from anything I have ever done. It's very different from what we had in the Church before—organizations with very pious names or social clubs. This is different.
>
> I think you should do this more often. I have never heard of a thing like this and I've always associated myself far away from the average priest. Now I feel much closer to him.

"Yes, it creates a better atmosphere around the Church. The Church is not that distant from me." "It breaks down the barrier to a priest, the stiff, formal image of the Church." "This gives a feeling of participation to the people." Such an informal atmosphere was very enjoyable and acceptable to the people where they felt free to talk and not be swayed in any direction. They valued such an atmosphere. It's good for people to "blow off steam"; at the same time they learn much. They discover kindred feelings in others. They have an image of a priest then, not the "census taker," the "financier making collections," not the "autocratic teacher," but someone who asks them questions seeking to understand them. It was an experiment that can find application in many ways, a means that can put life back into the Church, a new way for a priest to relate to his parishioners, perhaps the key to restructuring the whole parish, abandoning the organizational based parish to one without organization, but structured in this informal way.

[Appendix II]

Just an Afterthought

TO MANY, the consideration of the Latin language in the liturgy is now mostly academic. Following the Mass with a missal will be automatically conditioned by practical circumstances of active participation. We have added the following thoughts to help people rely less on the use of the missal and also to encourage them as they make the transition to the vernacular.

For many years, following the Mass with a missal has been considered the ideal method of attending Mass. Priests, nuns and laity encouraged its use and promoted its sale. In reality, placing the missal in the hands of the laity did not solve the difficult problems of boredom, inattention, or restlessness at Mass. There is no easy solution. People who walk around with ready-made answers really have no answers.

Sofia Cavaletti and Gianna Gobbi, in their book *Teaching Doctrine and Liturgy* say: "The use of the missal has been overstressed by many liturgists. After all, the person whose eyes are fastened on the missal cannot follow the movements of the priest which mean so much." [1]

My own experience in interviews substantiates this.

> You're kind of in your own world with the Missal.
>
> Before the recited Mass, I never followed the priest, I was usually way ahead or way behind. I'd be distracted terribly even though I would be reading. When I used to try to concentrate on the prayers in the missal, I wouldn't know what was going on at the altar. I was

[1] Staten Island, N. Y.: Alba House, 1964, p. 91.

> just reading by myself and not paying much attention to what was going on.
>
> When I am actively participating in the Mass, I feel a closeness to God. I don't get the same feeling when I use the missal.
>
> It makes me realize that this particular Mass isn't just for me as I do when I read the missal. The guy next to me has a part in it, and the guy next to him, too.

People felt very much alone at Mass when they used the missal. Others questioned the value of their prayers when using it, finding insufficient concentration and lack of ability to follow the Mass prayerfully. The following remarks were typical of their reactions:

> I've tried reading the missal, but somehow when I'm reading it I feel shut out from the participation completely.
>
> You can carry away something when you participate, whereas by using the missal it's like going to Mass and being a spectator.
>
> If I have a missal, it seems like I'm just reading and I don't have any feeling.
>
> I can't coordinate the use of the missal with the priest's actions at the altar.
>
> A lot of times I don't even see what the priest is doing at the altar even if I am following it with my missal. I'm not quite sure at what part the priest is.
>
> I can't keep up with the priest in my parish. If he gave me a two page start, he'd pass me up, so the missal is out.
>
> I feel rather alone and get lost. It seems the priest is tripping along on a bicycle and I just can't keep up with him.
>
> You certainly feel as though you are part of the Mass

> when you are participating. You feel as though you are up at the altar, too. As fas as reading the missal for that matter, you can read the missal at home and get the same effect as reading it at Mass silently. When you respond in church with the priest, you get a different feeling.

It was very difficult for me to accept the people's reaction to the missal. I frequently challenged the accuracy of their statements as in the following excerpt:

> You can do an awful lot of reading and very little praying.
>
> I would think you would have a better concentration using the missal.
>
> I don't know about you, but I could read and not think about what I'm reading. I can think about dishes, dinner or children and it is just as easy for me. I know. I've done it. But when you are actually participating, you hear the words as well as see them. How you can be remote under those circumstances I don't know. It's a physical impossibility.

As we made a study of people's feelings and attitudes at Mass, we found that for some the missal has become a real obstacle to participation, and becomes a substitute for the personal involvement which active participation encourages. A rigid attachment to any means of participation is destructive of a true spirit of worship. A kind of burial seems to take place among some people. Many lock themselves within the covers of a book and lose awareness of those about them—lose awareness of the very action at the altar.

Many of us have found great satisfaction in following the priest's action, word for word, thought for thought. I can recall my own rigid position on the use of the missal as far as Mass was concerned. I now realize, more than ever, the importance of asking the laity to share their experiences of participation at Mass.

Many will feel a nostalgia for the Latin as it was sung or said aloud. "The sound of the Latin is beautiful." "It's universal . . . that's the keypoint." "I was brought up with it." "The Mass won't be the same without it." "Learning the Latin was a challenge." "I'm in favor of the Latin. It's the language of the Church." Some will wonder why the change to English was made. If we must participate, why not in Latin? Would you find the change easier to make if you knew how people actually felt when they participated in Latin? Some have found the following insights helpful.

> The sound of Latin is beautiful, but there is no meaning, no feeling, no satisfaction; there's nothing there.
>
> I don't feel like I'm praying in church when I'm responding in Latin, I feel nothing. I'm trying hard to pronounce the words and that's all it is to me.
>
> How can I mean anything if I don't understand what I'm saying? I'm missing the whole idea of the Mass! I'm afraid to pronounce the words wrong—that's why I keep quiet. English is simple. I know what I'm talking about in English but to read it in Latin I can't put my heart and soul into it. In other words, those are just words to me.

The people raised a question about the Latin and analyzed it from two aspects, prayer and understanding. They spoke of a preoccupation with pronunciation of the words—of not being at ease with the language.

> I don't understand the words. Why say something I don't understand? It just doesn't get across at all—no value—doesn't mean a thing.
>
> When I'm praying in Latin, I'm just saying words. I don't know what I'm saying. I don't know what I'm doing, really, and I think it's better if we don't have it.

People like to understand what they're saying. Participating in a language they do not understand leaves them with no feeling—no satisfaction. Interest springs from understanding.

> Listen to the ballgame. You have to understand it, right? If I don't understand it, why should I watch it? The same goes for Latin and prayer.
>
> It might have some merit, the intentions are good, but for your own satisfaction. . . .
>
> When you're responding in English, you don't have to stop to read another page or line to know what you've said. You feel it more and are more aware of what you are saying than if you were responding in Latin. When I say the Our Father in Latin, I can say it with very little flaw, but I don't picture the meaning when I'm saying it.

It is very easy for a person in authority to say, "Well, the changes have been made, why bother about it anymore?"

Yes, in the Conciliar document the changes have been made. But in the hearts of many they have not been accepted. Many will experience such deep inner conflict as they struggle to accept the changes that they will actually feel lost at Mass.

It's most natural for a person to cling to the familiar—to reject the new because the accompanying feeling of insecurity is not a pleasant experience. We can all recall our reluctance to accept the new rules on fasting before Communion, the responsibility of saying "Amen" at just the right moment before receiving Holy Communion, and even more recently the changes made in the manner of Confession. These are real obstacles for many. What can we do to help other people as they struggle to accept?

When people read the experiences of others they will recognize themselves in them and will take courage from this feeling of kinship. Only then will the feelings of insecurity and fear be replaced by an enthusiasm springing from the realization that this is what the Mass really is.

A NOTE ON THE TYPE

IN WHICH THIS BOOK IS SET

This book is set in Garamond, a type face considered by many as one of the most successful ever introduced. Claude Garamond, the designer of these beautiful types, was a pupil of Geoffroy Tory, a leader of the Renaissance in France, a university professor, artist, designer and printer who set out to place French on an equal footing with Latin and Greek as a language o fculture. Garamond's evenness of color throughout the font is highly appreciated by book designers. The moderately strong fine lines tend to soften the effect, which is decidedly agreeable to many. This book composed by Wickersham Printing Company, Lancaster, Pa., and bound by Moore & Company of Baltimore. The typography and design of this book are by Howard N. King.